Digital Connections
in the **Classroom**

DAVID MARCOVITZ

International Society for Technology in Education
EUGENE, OREGON • WASHINGTON, DC

Digital Connections *in the* Classroom

DAVID MARCOVITZ

Director of Book Publishing: *Courtney Burkholder*
Acquisitions Editor: *Jeff V. Bolkan*
Production Editors: *Tina Wells, Lynda Gansel*
Production Coordinators: *Emily Reed, Rachel Williams*
Graphic Designer: *Signe Landin*
Copy Editor: *Kathy Hamman*
Proofreader: *Anna Drexler*
Cover Design, Book Design, and Production: *Kathy Sturtevant*

Library of Congress Cataloging-in-Publication Data

Marcovitz, David M.
 Digital connections in the classroom / David Marcovitz — First Edition
    pages cm
 Includes bibliographical references and index.
 ISBN 978-1-56484-316-6
 1. Educational technology. I. Title.
 LB1028.3.M375 2012
 371.33—dc23

                                                              2012007710

First Edition
ISBN: 978-1-56484-316-6
Printed in the United States of America

Cover Art (background): © iStockphoto.com/Natal'ya Bondarenko
ISTE® is a registered trademark of the International Society for Technology in Education.

About ISTE

The International Society for Technology in Education (ISTE) is the trusted source for professional development, knowledge generation, advocacy, and leadership for innovation. ISTE is the premier membership association for educators and education leaders engaged in improving teaching and learning by advancing the effective use of technology in PK–12 and teacher education.

Home of ISTE's annual conference and exposition, the ISTE leadership conference, and the widely adopted NETS, ISTE represents more than 100,000 professionals worldwide. We support our members with information, networking opportunities, and guidance as they face the challenge of transforming education. To find out more about these and other ISTE initiatives, visit our website at www.iste.org.

As part of our mission, ISTE Book Publishing works with experienced educators to develop and produce practical resources for classroom teachers, teacher educators, and technology leaders. Every manuscript we select for publication is carefully peer-reviewed and professionally edited. We value your feedback on this book and other ISTE products. Email us at books@iste.org.

International Society for Technology in Education
Washington, DC, Office:
    1710 Rhode Island Ave. NW, Suite 900, Washington, DC 20036-3132
Eugene, Oregon, Office:
    180 West 8th Ave., Suite 300, Eugene, OR 97401-2916
Order Desk: 1.800.336.5191
Order Fax: 1.541.302.3778
Customer Service: orders@iste.org
Book Publishing: books@iste.org
Book Sales and Marketing: booksmarketing@iste.org
Web: www.iste.org

About the Author

 **David Marcovitz** is associate professor in the School of Education and director of the Graduate Program in Educational Technology at Loyola University Maryland. He received a doctorate in educational technology from the University of Illinois at Urbana-Champaign, where he studied support for technology in elementary schools. He has taught computer applications and computer programming at the high school level and has worked as a technology specialist in a high school. Prior to coming to Loyola University, Marcovitz taught in the educational technology program at Florida Atlantic University. He was hired by Loyola in 1997 to develop a Masters Program in Educational Technology; he now coordinates the program and teaches many of its classes. Marcovitz is the author of several articles and book chapters, as well as the book *Powerful PowerPoint for Educators*. He received the Microsoft Community Contributor Award in 2012 and the Microsoft PowerPoint Most Valuable Professional Award from 2005 through 2010.

Acknowledgment

Although my name appears on the cover of this book, I couldn't have written it without a lot of help. I would like to thank my wife, Emily, and children, Ella and Ada, for putting up with my long hours of writing even while on vacation. I would like to thank my department chair, Dr. Peter Rennert-Ariev, for helping me shift my teaching schedule so I could have some blocks of time to write. I would like to thank my graduate assistant, Linda Daywalt, for helping me with some of the background research for the book. I would like to thank all the people who contributed to the book; their real examples bring the ideas in the book to life. Finally, I would like to thank my students. Many of the observations and ideas in this book are things that I have learned from them over the years. Most of my students are teaching in K–12 classrooms, and it is enlightening for me to see how they use technology to motivate their students to learn. I introduce my students to new tools and ideas, and they take them in new directions, in turn teaching me how they work in the real world. I also want to thank them for reading many of the chapters in this book (even though they were assignments) and giving me useful feedback on them.

Dedication

This book is dedicated to my students and to the students of my students, who will shape the 21st century.

Contents

CHAPTER SEVEN

Copyright and the Free Web 131

CHAPTER EIGHT

Digital Citizenship in a Dangerous World 159

CHAPTER NINE

Basics of Web Design and HTML

Introduction

This book is intended for current and future teachers and other students of education who want to find exciting ways to incorporate technology into the classroom. It is aimed at K–12 teachers, but I am sure some of the information will be valuable at the post-secondary level as well. It can be used as a stand-alone book for someone interested in learning how to use the Internet in the classroom, and it can be used as a textbook for an undergraduate or graduate class in educational technology. In fact, I wrote it because I couldn't find a suitable textbook to use for a graduate class that I teach at Loyola University Maryland, Digital Communication in the Classroom. This class is part of a Masters Program in Educational Technology that follows the ISTE standards for Technology Facilitation and is reviewed by ISTE as part of our accreditation process (see NCATE, www.ncate.org).

Nine Broad Topics

This book describes ways that digital communication and the Internet can be used in the classroom. Each chapter's topic really could be an entire book, but the chapters provide enough information to help a current or future teacher develop a firm grasp of the concepts, enough of a grasp to try using these tools in the classroom. The real lessons won't be learned from a book but from actually thinking about the material, trying out some tools, writing some lessons, and using them in the classroom.

Because the topics of the book are centered around a very large theme, you may find that some topics relating to the theme don't appear in the book. I don't, for example, cover uses of newer communication devices, such as cell phones and tablets (even though I love my iPad). Many teachers are doing interesting things with those devices, and I'm sure that books and blogs and wikis are cropping up to give you ideas for using them to enhance your teaching. Those devices will make some types of instruction discussed in this book easier, and they may inspire you to try new projects that aren't covered in this book.

Additionally, some of you will find that some of the chapters don't fit your needs. Most of the chapters stand on their own, so feel free to skip any that don't meet your needs. I wouldn't want someone to slog through, for example, a web page creation chapter and hate me for it. I think a class web page is important, and I explain why in the chapter, but if it's not right for you, skip it. If it's not right for your students, don't assign it to them.

The book consists of nine chapters: Internet basics, critical information literacy, Wikipedia, telecollaborative projects, Web 2.0, strategies for searching the web, copyright and free resources on the web, digital citizenship, and basic web page design.

Chapter One covers the basics of the Internet. Chapter Two focuses on critical information literacy. Critical information literacy is about helping our students to become deep thinkers about what they find on the web: getting beyond accepting what they read at face value and then moving beyond making simplistic yes/no judgments about sites they encounter.

Chapter Three is a short chapter about Wikipedia. Wikipedia is a much-maligned resource. The Wikipedia chapter will help you think about how that resource (and others like it) can and cannot be useful.

Chapter Four is about telecollaborative projects. You will find resources to help you break down the walls of your classroom to communicate with a wide range of people, including students in other classrooms, to widen your students' learning and help them gain perspectives that are not present within any single classroom.

The term Web 2.0 has become one of the hottest terms in schools. Chapter Five defines Web 2.0 and explains many ways Web 2.0 tools can be used to increase communication and collaboration inside and outside your classroom.

The web is full of many resources, but they are not always easy to find. Chapter Six provides a framework for thinking about searching the web for information. Some search tools that take you beyond Google are also introduced.

Finding appropriate media, such as pictures and sounds, on the web can be difficult. When copyright is considered, you might find that your ability to use the media that you find is severely limited. Chapter Seven describes tools designed to help you find media that is legal to use and encourages you to join the Creative Commons community that makes that possible.

Many schools and instructors are hesitant to use the Internet to its fullest potential because we all know that the web can be a dangerous place. Chapter Eight puts the dangers into perspective and helps you weigh the risks of using the Internet against the risks of not using it. That chapter discusses how we can teach digital citizenship and how we can appropriately use tools, such as filters and acceptable use policies, to maintain a safe environment without locking our students out from important learning opportunities.

The book concludes with Chapter Nine, a brief introduction to web page design. The web is no longer simply about gathering information. It is also about producing information. Having a firm grasp of the tools required to produce information on the web is important. Chapter Nine gives you an introduction to those tools.

I hope that this book will help you think beyond the walls of your classroom and find new ways to help your students learn. Some of this book is about motivation and meeting your students where they are, but mostly it is about new ways of thinking and collaborating and learning that can't be done (or can't be done easily) without the new tools and opportunities that the web makes possible.

CHAPTER ONE

Internet Basics

What does your classroom have, and what is it missing? Are all the resources your students need for learning contained in your classroom or in your school? Are there possibilities beyond the school walls for tools, resources, and collaborators? The Internet brings you a wide range of tools, resources, and collaborators. Though it can't always replace real field trips and face-to-face discussions, sometimes using the Internet's tools can expand what we instructors do in ways that make our students' learning experiences much more powerful than what we and they are capable of doing without it.

History of the Internet

The Internet was started around the 1960s as a project of the Defense Advanced Research Project Agency (DARPA) as a way to connect computers used for scientific research. It is really a network of networks that started with a small number of computers, mostly at universities and government agencies, and has expanded to billions of computers. Aside from the physical connections (the wires that connect machines), the Internet is a set of protocols and standards that allow all the software, computers, and networks to interact.

Nowadays, most people think of the Internet and the World Wide Web (or just the web) as the same thing, but they are not. The web is really an application that runs on the Internet. Your browser has certain ways of communicating with web servers to bring you information from faraway places. Many other applications run on the Internet. Although you might use a browser to read your email (via web access), email is an application that is different from the web and has been around much longer than the web. Your email system communicates with other email addresses through a different set of protocols from those the web uses. Many other applications use the Internet—File Transfer Protocol (FTP), Gopher (a menu-based information system that was the precursor to the web), Network News Transfer Protocol (NNTP), and others—but the web and email are the two main applications that you see. Just think of the Internet as the all-encompassing network itself, with the web and email as applications that use the network to move around information.

Prior to the web, most communication on the Internet was clumsy and technical. Other than email, doing much of anything required a working knowledge of a set of technical commands. The web changed our Internet interactions from those complicated commands into a much easier graphical user interface. Rather than typing a command to find something, you now click on links.

Just like some of the other Internet applications mentioned, the web is really a protocol: Hypertext Transfer Protocol (HTTP). You might recognize the acronym because most URLs (uniform resource locator or web address) start with *http://* followed by the address. The main language of the web is Hypertext Markup Language (HTML). Pages are created in HTML and put on servers. Users who want to read those pages use programs called browsers to get the pages from the servers. The most common browsers include Firefox, Internet Explorer, Opera, Chrome, and Safari. You probably use one or more of these, but there are many others, including browsers that read text to the blind and browsers designed to squeeze web pages down to the size of cell phone screens.

When you open your browser, you can go to any page on the web by typing in its URL. Your browser then uses HTTP to send a signal over the Internet to the server where the page is located. The server sends the page (mostly in the form of HTML) back to your browser. Your browser interprets the HTML and shows the page to you. The server could be in the same room or on the other side of the world. Although the details are a lot more complicated, this is most of what you need to know. The browser and the server (and all points between) take care of the technical details for you.

Browsers

The browser is the main portal into the web. Generally, when you are looking at a web page, you are operating within a browser. Currently, the two most popular browsers are Internet Explorer and Firefox, but there are many other browsers in use. Here is a partial list of popular browsers:

Internet Explorer
http://windows.microsoft.com/en-US/Internet-explorer/downloads/ie

> This is the browser that comes bundled with Microsoft Windows, and it is only available for computers that use Windows (older versions were once available for Macintosh computers as well).

Firefox
http://www.mozilla.com/firefox (*or* www.mozilla.com/firefox *or* mozilla.com)

> This is an open source browser managed by Mozilla Corporation. It is available for computers that use Windows, Macintosh, and Linux and for Android cell phones.

Safari

http://www.apple.com/safari (*or* www.apple.com/safari)

> This was created by Apple, so it is mainly used on Apple products (such as Macs, iPhones, and iPads), and there is also a version for Windows.

Google Chrome

http://www.google.com/chrome (*or* www.google.com/chrome)

> This is the browser developed by Google. It runs on Mac, Windows, and Linux.

Opera

http://www.opera.com (*or* www.opera.com)

> This was created by Opera Software and is available for Windows, Mac, Linux, and for many cell phones.

Mosaic and Netscape Navigator

> Mosaic was the first popular graphical web browser, developed at the National Center for Supercomputing Applications at the University of Illinois in 1992 and 1993. Netscape was a commercial venture based on Mosaic. Neither browser is available today, but they are mentioned here because they represent the beginning of the web.

For basic features, most browsers work the same way. For most of your purposes, you won't notice much of a difference from one browser to the next. Browsers are updated all the time, so as soon as a new feature is added to one browser, many of the other browsers add it to later versions. Additionally, all the browsers mentioned above are free, so if you want to see if one browser works better than another, just download it and try it out.

HTML Codes

The main feature of browsers is interpreting HTML code (see Chapter Nine) and displaying it on the screen in a graphical format. This means that designers can create pages with a variety of technology tools that people on different computers can view. There are HTML standards, and browsers generally follow these standards. This means that if designers follow these standards, a web page in one browser will look the same as a web page on another browser. However, this isn't true 100% of the time as some designers like to use nonstandard features of HTML that are only supported by some browsers. This is a good reason to keep more than one browser on your computer: if something doesn't look right on one browser, try it on another browser.

Plug-Ins

Of course, the web has gotten more complicated than using simple HTML commands that tell the browser to put this picture here and that text there. Browsers support JavaScript, Flash video, embedded PDF files, and much more. Most of this is supported with plug-ins (also known as add-ons or add-ins). Some of these come with browsers, while others need to be downloaded and updated regularly. Here are a few plug-ins that are perhaps the most common:

Adobe Flash Player
http://get.adobe.com/flashplayer

Flash Player is one of the most widely used plug-ins. Developers can create videos and interactive features using Adobe Flash.

Adobe Reader
http://get.adobe.com/reader

Adobe Reader is often used as a separate application, but the plug-in sometimes will be used to view PDF (Portable Document Format) files directly in the browser without opening a separate application.

Apple QuickTime
http://www.apple.com/quicktime/download

QuickTime is a multimedia (mainly used for videos) format that is popular on the web, and this plug-in allows QuickTime files to be displayed on web pages.

Microsoft Silverlight
http://www.microsoft.com/getsilverlight

Silverlight is a Microsoft platform that can add many video and interactive capabilities to websites and is used by many of Microsoft's online tools.

Plug-ins are not always interchangeable. You generally need the specific plug-in for the kind of content you are viewing on the web. Fortunately, in most cases, when you come to a website that requires a plug-in, you will be given the opportunity to download it and install it. Alternatively, you can go to the websites just listed and download and install the common plug-ins before you get to a website. Plug-ins work behind the scenes with the browser so frequently you won't even notice you have them; you will only notice you don't have them when some content does not show up in your browser.

The downside of plug-ins is that the web is complicated and more likely to work differently on different computers and different browsers (and sometimes not work at all in certain browsers). The upside is that many more advanced and interactive features, such as a variety of video formats and Web 2.0 applications (see Chapter Five), are available to make the web a much more powerful and interactive experience.

Reading a Web Address

When you look at a URL, you will notice that it is a series of pieces separated by periods (each pronounced *dot*). To understand the URL, you can look at it from right to left. For example, http://www.loyola.edu usually appears as www.loyola.edu (pronounced *W-W-W-dot-Loyola-dot-E-D-U*). The far right of the address is *.edu*. That is a top-level domain reserved for educational institutions (mostly colleges and universities). Other common top-level domains are .com for private companies, .net for private companies that have more to do with the Internet, .org for organizations, and .gov for government sites. Note that .edu and .gov are fairly tightly controlled, but the other domains are not, so anyone can get a .org, .com, or .net address. For example, I am not a private company, but I own the domain marcovitz.com, and disney.org simply redirects your browser to the Walt Disney Corporation .com site. Some resources on website evaluation suggest using the top-level domain as a factor in whether the site is reliable. This is not a good idea because of the lack of control of many top-level domains and because some top-level domains include information from a wide range of users related to the company or organization using the domain. For example, many universities give space to faculty, staff, and students for personal use under the .edu domain.

In addition to the top-level domains that reflect (more or less) the type of information found there, each country has a top-level domain. Anything you find ending in .us is likely from the United States, while anything you find ending .uk is probably from the United Kingdom. Each country has its own top-level domain, but a few countries make money by selling addresses in their domains rather than reserving them for sites in their own countries. For example, addresses ending in .tv are more likely to be about television than from the island nation of Tuvalu.

Aside from the original top-level domains (.com, .net, .org, .edu, .gov, and .mil) and the country-specific top-level domains, the Internet Corporation for Assigned Numbers and Names (ICANN), the international organization that controls top-level domains, has added several new domains (for example, .aero, .biz, .coop, .museum, .name, .info, and .pro). In June 2011, ICANN approved making available almost anything as a domain name (called generic top-level domains). As of this writing, the proposal is in the process of being implemented, but it is not yet fully implemented. Applications were being accepted through April 2012. If I had applied by the deadline, I could have registered the .marcovitz domain (instead of relying on marcovitz.com), except that the cost of a new top-level domain is $185,000 plus $25,000 per year (as opposed to the few dollars per year I spend to keep marcovitz.com).

After looking at the top-level domain, move to the left to get more specific. In www.loyola.edu, the *.edu* tells you that it is probably the domain of a university, and the next slot to the left (*loyola*, for example) tells you which institution (Loyola University Maryland). To the left of that might be a more specific part of the institution, such as a department, or it might be the machine name of the specific server. Many servers are named www (for World Wide Web), but that is just a common convention. The machine names can be anything that the institution wants to name them. You are likely to find the main server of an institution named www, but that is not a requirement. When the web was new, the main website of the Massachusetts Institute of Technology (MIT) was web.mit.edu while www.mit.edu was for a student organization on campus. Now, both web.mit.edu and www.mit.edu take you to the main MIT server. For most URLs, you can leave off the www at the beginning of the address, and you will be taken to the main server.

Each machine on the Internet has an IP (Internet Protocol) address, which is a series of numbers that help direct information to that machine, but you rarely type a series

■ DISSECTING A URL

I used to teach at Poinciana High School. The URL of the school's main server is www.phs.osceola.k12.fl.us. Reading from right to left, you see *.us* (the top-level domain) because it is in the United States. Then comes *fl* for Florida, *k12* because it is a school in Florida, and *osceola* because it is in the Osceola County School District. Finally, *phs* stands for Poinciana High School, and the main machine is *www*. Each slot in the URL, going from right to left, from the top-level domain to the machine name, becomes more specific.

of numbers in order to get to any machine. This is all handled by the Domain Name System. You type a URL (using words), and a domain name server (which is like a big electronic phone book) looks up the number and tells your browser to go to that IP address. This happens behind the scenes, so you rarely have to worry about it.

From the Internet to Web 2.0 and Beyond

Back in the old days, we had Web 0.0 (that was really before the web at all). There were some pretty good email applications, but just about anything else you wanted to do was hard. Many things required some technical knowledge, and most people didn't use the Internet, or if they did, they just used simple email or chat tools. Also, everything you saw was text. In the early 1990s, Web 1.0 came about. This was a graphical interface to the Internet. You still needed technical skills to create things beyond simple emails or chats, but you needed very little skill to access information. Web 1.0, for most users, is all about accessing information.

As you try to get information from the web, you will get to web pages in one of five ways:

1. You know the address and type it in your browser.

2. You click on a link from some other place.

3. You go to your list of favorites or bookmarks for someplace you have been before.

4. You search based on keywords using a search engine.

5. You guess the URL (many are obvious variations of the name of the company or organization).

The web can be a great source of information. Some refer to it as a giant library. However, unlike libraries, it is disorganized and full of a lot of junk. In some ways, the web is more like Jorge Luis Borges's imagined short story, "Library of Babel" ("La Biblioteca de Babel," 1941), which contains every possible combination of characters formed into books, than a regular library (Bruce, 2000). In a Web 1.0 mindset, your primary goal is to get information created by others. You can use the five techniques above to find information.

Chapter Two, Critical Information Literacy, provides more ideas about how to think about the information you find. In Chapter Six, Searching the Web, you'll learn more tips and tricks for finding information. As teachers, one of our primary goals must be to help our students think about and think with the information they find. It is not enough simply to make yes/no judgments about web pages. We need to help our students understand the wide range of facts, opinions, and insights offered on the web, whether from good sites, bad sites, or sites that can't be neatly packaged into good or bad. Then, we can show our students how they can become "hyperreaders" (Burbules & Callister, 2000), interacting with what they find.

The world has shifted from a Web 1.0 mindset to a Web 2.0 mindset. In a Web 2.0 mindset, the goal is to create, communicate, and interact with others. It's not just about what you can find; instead, it's about what you can share and what you can create together. Much of what you might want to do to create and interact was possible with Web 1.0 tools, but it was too difficult for most people to do. In fact, the kind of hyper-reading that Burbules and Callister (2000) discuss (long before Web 2.0 existed) is exactly the kind of interaction that Web 2.0 makes easier (see Chapter Five, Web 2.0). This kind of interaction isn't just about motivating students (it's more than just "fun"); it's about working with others to expand our classrooms and our thinking (see Chapter Four, Telecollaborative Projects). Web 2.0 tools make the collaboration easy. Twenty years ago, videoconferencing was either expensive or flaky or both, so it was rarely done. Today, free or low-cost options such as Skype are fairly reliable. Twenty years ago, joint work on a document involved complex computer-supported-collaborative-work (CSCW) tools. Today, pop up a document on Google Docs or a wiki, and share it with others so they can make changes. It's not that we couldn't videoconference or work collaboratively before—it's that only the geekiest among us would attempt these activities.

Now that the tools make it easier to collaborate, how does that affect the classroom? Think about what your classroom is missing. If your answer is nothing, you're not thinking hard enough. You might be missing expertise. You might find other instructors or tech support professionals who are willing to share their expertise. Few people would fly around the world to spend 10 minutes in your classroom, but if the visit only took 10 minutes via Skype, you might find a geologist or electrical engineer or zookeeper who would be willing to speak to your class.

As an instructor working by yourself, you might be missing large quantities of data. A quick survey shared with 100 classrooms around the world might do the trick (check out the Tooth Tally Project, www.toothtally.com). Now, imagine that data isn't just quantity but quality. You might be missing data from different geographic regions, such as first-person observations of the migration of butterflies (see Journey North: A Global Study of Wildlife Migration and Seasonal Change, www.learner.org/jnorth). Using this tool, you can follow the migration by collecting your own data and using the data collected by other classrooms in other areas. To deepen your understanding of the power of digital connections, see Box 1.1, Metcalfe's Law.

Box 1.1

Metcalfe's Law

Metcalfe's law suggests that the usefulness of a network is related to the square of the number of people and/or machines connected to it (n^2). If you have a network with one other person, it's slightly useful. If you have two other people, you can connect to each of them, and they can connect to each other person (3 people × 2 connections each = 6). If you have three other people, you can connect to each of them, and they can talk to each of the other people (4 people × 3 connections each = 12). If you have a million people on the network, you have a possibility of a 1,000,000 × 999,999, or about a trillion useful connections. As the number of people on the Internet has grown, the network has gotten more and more useful. Does that mean that one more person posting videos of his cat adds that much value? Probably not. However, when the store down the street, the rare record dealer in South Carolina, the government agency that coordinates farmers' markets, and the classroom in India that wants to share stories with you are all connected to the network, the value builds rapidly. Just like a million hits on Google aren't necessarily better than a thousand hits, the more that are available, the more likely it is that you can make useful connections.

The huge number of connections now available on the Internet makes a feature called the "long tail" a reality. This was described by Chris Anderson in his October 2004 article in *Wired* (see www.wired.com/wired/archive/12.10/tail.html). A real-world example of the long-tail principle in action is the book business. Go into a typical physical bookstore, and you'll see a pretty good selection of recent titles along with some of the most popular titles from the last few years at best. Visit an online bookstore, and you'll probably find nearly every title still in print and, via the bookstore's network of sellers, most titles that are out of print.

You might be missing cultural diversity, and the power of connection might not be in data but in perspective. Using ePals (www.epals.com), iEARN (www.iearn.org), and the Flat Classroom Project (www.flatclassroomproject.org) can give you the power to connect and collaborate with classrooms around the world. Tools and projects like these tear down the walls of the classroom, making learning more meaningful and more authentic. The Industrial Age lasted a long time, but the Information Age was short-lived, as we quickly learned that information is only part of what we need. Digital age learning is about collaborating to transform information into knowledge and understanding. Great teachers do a lot of that with just the tools available inside the classroom, but the classroom walls are limiting, and a wealth of tools are available to do so much more.

The rest of this book takes you through a wide range of uses of the Internet in the classroom, from Web 1.0 to Web 2.0 and digital age learning. Think of the web as an information tool, but don't stop there. Think of it is as a collaboration tool and as a thinking tool. Your students will need specific skills to navigate the complexity of the Internet, and they will need access to the tools of the Internet to go beyond information gathering. This book will help you take your students there. It's not the end, but the beginning of a journey through knowledge, understanding, and collaboration— the skills of today and tomorrow.

References

Bruce, B. C. (2000, February). Credibility of the web: Why we need dialectical reading. *Journal of Philosophy of Education, 34*(1), 97–109. Also in P. Standish & N. Blake (Eds.), *Enquiries at the interface: Philosophical problems of online education* (pp. 107-122). Oxford, UK: Blackwell. [DOI: 10.1111/1467-9752.00158] Retrieved December 22, 2010, from http://www.ideals.illinois.edu/bitstream/handle/2142/13425/credibility.pdf

Borges, J. L. (1941). "La Biblioteca de Babel," cited in this article, has been translated into English and is in *Labyrinths, Selected Stories and Other Writings* by Jorge Luis Borges (1899–1986).

Burbules, N. C., & Callister, T. A., Jr. (2000). *Watch IT: The risks and promises of information technologies for education.* Boulder, CO: Westview Press.

CHAPTER TWO

Critical Information Literacy

What do we want our students to be able to do when they encounter a website? This is a complex question. In the ideal situation, we want them to think deeply about the site, analyze it for accuracy and biases, and think about its relationship to the broader context of knowledge in the domain being examined. But sometimes I just want to know who won the ball game last night. In other words, there is a great difference between the need to find a tidbit of information and the need to understand a topic in depth. By our very nature, humans are "cognitive misers" (a term coined by Fiske & Taylor, 1991). That is, we do not take all available information, analyze it carefully, and come to the best decision. We automatically screen out some irrelevant information and even eliminate some relevant information. "The idea is that people are limited in their capacity to process information, so they take shortcuts whenever they can. ... People adopt strategies to simplify complex problems; the strategies may not be normatively correct or produce normatively correct answers, but they emphasize efficiency" (Fiske & Taylor, 1991, p. 13).

When looking up the score of the ball game, I might not want to know the details of the game, the background of the players, the social context of sports in this and other countries, or the history of racism in sports. I also don't care about the ownership of http://espn.go.com, the network's bias for or against some sports, background on the controversy of reporting player statistics, or other details not related to the score. Additionally, I don't want to spend a lot of time looking for the answer, so I might try a quick way to find the answer. If it is too difficult or time consuming, I'll probably give up.

What if I want to find out what happened last night in the West Bank? I might find some facts about a military raid, such as who attacked whom, how many were killed, and so on. But in this case, even the question is full of issues simply by using the term "West Bank." From there, a whole line of questioning can be raised about the history of the region from a wide range of viewpoints. When I pose my original question, I might not be interested in a deeper exploration of the issues in the Middle East, and I might be a cognitive miser and grab the first source that can tell me some basic facts about the event. However, superficial facts don't give me a full picture of what really happened. I need the skills to dig deeply.

The problem is that many of our and our students' encounters with the web are closer to finding the score of the game (or the capital of Germany) than trying to make sense of the complexities of an issue or digging deeply into a domain of knowledge. By a very early age, our students become quite good at finding the quick fact and have little practice using the web as a resource to help them think deeply about an issue. The danger is that our students will not have the skills to assess and navigate websites and think deeply about issues they encounter. The goal of Critical Information Literacy is to equip them with these skills. We know that our students won't use them all the time or even most of the time—they will continue to be cognitive misers even in situations that call for deeper thinking—but they are important skills to have, and students are unlikely to pick them up without our help.

Burbules and Callister (2000) discuss three types of readers of the web: browsers, users, and hyperreaders (pp. 54–55). Browsers are simply looking around, stumbling on whatever might interest them. Users are looking for specific information. Hyperreaders are engaging in a dialogue with the text, and in the Web 2.0 world are interacting and altering the text. Although Burbules and Callister wrote before Web 2.0, much of their writing anticipates Web 2.0, and specific Web 2.0 technologies simply make it easier for hyperreaders to have the kind of relationship with the web that they envisioned.

Burbules and Callister (2000) also place an intermediate category between user and hyperreader: the critical user. Most instruction about the web is geared to helping our students become critical users. Critical users take a skeptical stance regarding the information they find. They know to look for such things as authority, accuracy, objectivity, currency, and coverage (see Box 2.1, Evaluating Information Sources). Critical users might be equipped with checklists (see, for example, the University of Chicago's "Evaluate a Web Site Checklist": http://cuip.uchicago.edu/wit/2000/curriculum/homeroommodules/assessEdSites/evalchecklist.htm). The focus of critical users generally is to make a yes/no judgment about a site: Is this a good or bad site? Kaufmann (1977) and Bruce (2000) refer to this type of reading as the "agnostic mode." Bruce (2000) describes the agnostic mode of reading the web:

> In a fashion that is a priori appropriate in the information age, agnostic readers adopt a technical stance toward web quality. They acknowledge that there are both good and bad resources, and so develop schemes for finding good sites and separating one from the other. The agnostic mode entails attention to developing and finding better tools for accessing the web, to conducting effective web searches, and to evaluating the quality of websites. (p. 104)

In many cases, this critical, skeptical, or agnostic stance to web resources is good enough. But Bruce (2000) argues that some of the time we need to go beyond that viewpoint and become "dialectical readers." The problem is that reading the web is not always about looking up information. Sometimes it is about entering a deep relationship with a domain of knowledge. Sometimes it is a journey with no clear beginning and end.

Box 2.1

Evaluating Information Sources

Many sources have adapted the criteria for evaluating traditional informa-tion sources to web sources. For more detailed discussions of this topic, look at Beck, 1997 (specifically http://lib.nmsu.edu/instruction/evalcrit.html or http://kathyschrock.net/abceval/5ws.htm). Here is a simple guide, based on main evaluation criteria categories from the website by Susan E. Beck at the New Mexico State University Library:

Authority. Who wrote the site? By what authority does the author speak? Does the author have credentials or other signs of expertise? On websites, it is often difficult to find the author as the person's name is not always listed.

Accuracy. Is the information accurate? Without expertise, you might not be able to judge the accuracy completely, but you might find discrep-ancies between what the site says and what you know. Alternatively, you can look for the names of fact checkers or editors who might have verified the information.

Objectivity. Is the information biased, or does it seem to take one particular viewpoint while ignoring others? Many sites on the web are created with the sole purpose of swaying your opinion.

Currency. Is the information up to date? This might not matter for a topic that is historical, but for a current topic, the difference between a few days and a few months or years can be large. On the web, it is often difficult to find a date, and, when you do find a date, it is not always clear what it means. It could be the date the information was created, the date the information was placed on the web, the date the information was last changed, the date the information was last thoroughly reviewed, the copyright date, or today's date.

Coverage. Does the site cover a wide range of thought on the topic? This is often the most difficult question, especially when you don't already know much about the topic. Also, should a site be rejected because it is not comprehensive, or can you combine the information from one limited site with the information from other limited sites to create your own "coverage" of the topic?

Bruce describes searching for information on the web as an exciting journey:

> For certain kinds of queries, my search is far from a simple lookup. Instead, it appears to be part of the general process of inquiry, which is tentative and fallible. There is no absolute starting point, nor is there any sure way to reach the end, assuming such a point exists. I need to muster all my resources for critical thinking in order to navigate my way through the web, but in the process may reap enormous benefits. (2000, p. 106)

If I want to look up information about the Middle East, I certainly can find many credible sites with historical facts. But simply looking at when the state of Israel was founded, the dates of the various wars, or even a variety of facts about the British Mandate only begins to touch the surface. In the agnostic stance, we might reach official and unofficial Hamas sites like www.pmo.gov.ps, www.hamasinfo.net, or www.qassam.ps and try to make judgments about whether to accept or reject the sites.

As a dialectical reader, we would want to engage with a site and figure out where it fits within the larger domain of knowledge. It would tell us different things from other sites, some of which may or may not be factual. As a critical reader, we might choose to reject it. As a dialectical reader, we want to be able to understand it within the multi-dimensional landscape I refer to as the domain of knowledge about the Middle East. Figure 2.1 is an oversimplified map of the domain of knowledge of the Arab-Israeli conflict. It is not meant to be all-inclusive (that would require a much larger page) or accurate (in regard to the position of terms), but it is meant to give you the sense of what a map of a domain of knowledge might look like. You could draw a domain of knowledge like this or use mind-mapping software such as Inspiration, Kidspiration, or bubbl.us (http://bubbl.us).

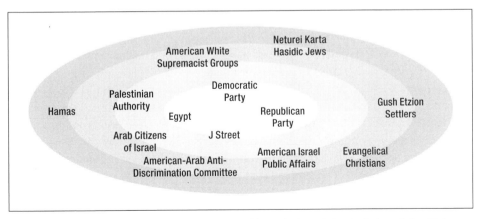

Figure 2.1 Oversimplified map of the domain of knowledge of the Arab-Israeli Conflict. Sources closest to the center represent more "balanced" sites.

The more "balanced" sites in Figure 2.1 are closest to the center; those along the edge/fringe are more partisan. It is critical to note that being partisan does not necessarily mean that a person or group is wrong; a person who is partisan is passionately dedicated to a particular cause or political party.

You might be thinking that there is a lot to understand about the Middle East, but most topics are far less controversial. Although it is true that some domains of knowledge are far less complex and controversial than the Middle East, a dialectical reading of the web will find depth to almost any topic you explore.

As I am writing this book, a new website, www.sharecare.com, has just been launched. This site provides expert information about a wide range of health issues by providing answers to questions. Some contributors, such as physician Mehmet Oz (Dr. Oz), are respected medical experts. Other contributors are site sponsors, such as Walgreens. Although the answers provided by sponsors are marked on the site, many readers will ignore the marking and not realize that the answers are marketing messages. Is the information provided by marketers necessarily bad or slanted? According to a simple checklist, it might lose out on the question of authority or the question of bias. But if the question is about a particular medication, perhaps the pharmacy is the right place to go for an answer.

Other sites present interesting challenges, especially for younger web readers. Part of the issue revolves around a lack of background knowledge. Many checklists use the term "coverage" as one of the criteria for evaluating sites. That is, does the site being evaluated cover the range of facts and opinions about this topic? Two thoughts come to mind: Why would you expect one site to cover everything around a topic, and how would you know?

Earlier, I suggested that there is value in looking at the Hamas website. I would never expect to find all sides of the issues of the Middle East there or on any single website. However, I wouldn't expect to find Hamas' viewpoint widely represented on many other sites, even sites that appear to provide a balanced perspective. Expecting one site to cover the entire range of facts and opinions on a topic is unrealistic. As for the second question, without extensive background knowledge of a topic, I wouldn't have any basis for judging how thoroughly a site covers a topic. Bruce (2000) gives the example of the epic poem *Beowulf.* In 2000, his search resulted in tens of thousands of results. Today, the same search gives over six million results. If all I want is a basic plot and background summary (little more than a quick look up of facts), many of the sites will do just fine. However, to begin to understand the controversies regarding the Christian and pagan elements of the story, I have to dig deeper. Without background knowledge, I might not be aware of the controversies until I start digging, and I might come across a site from one side of the debate and have no idea that its coverage of the topic is limited.

Fake Websites

Many fake websites have popped up. Some of these sites have been created for the purpose of website evaluation or just for fun. Although the sites are obviously fake, an interesting exercise can be built around seeing how many of your students will believe them to be legitimate. The All About Explorers website (www.allaboutexplorers.com) is an example of a site created for the specific purpose of teaching website evaluation. An example of the information about Christopher Columbus from the site is as follows:

> In 1942 he set sail with three ships, the Nina, Pinta and Santa Maria and about 90 men. The voyage was so much easier than sailing east. On October 12, 1942 Columbus landed on an island southeast of Florida. He claimed this island for Spain and named it the Indies, since he thought he had landed in India. He named the native people of the island Indians. The Indians were excited by the newcomers and their gadgets. They especially enjoyed using their cell phones and desktop computers.

We would hope our students would have enough background knowledge to see this as full of incorrect "facts," but many don't. The site is designed professionally and is easy to read, making it a good site to introduce the idea of skepticism. The site also provides exercises and lesson plans for teachers.

Here is a resource list of fake websites:

All About Explorers
www.allaboutexplorers.com

Facts About the Civil War
www.wiredsafety.org/wiredlearning/Evaluation/notetaking/sites/civilwar.htm

Dihydrogen Monoxide
www.dhmo.org

Haggis Hunt
http://haggishunt.scotsman.com

Mankato, Minnesota
http://city-mankato.us

Sellafield Zoo
www.brookview.karoo.net/Sellafield_Zoo/

The Pacific Northwest Tree Octopus
http://zapatopi.net/treeoctopus/

Pop! The First Male Pregnancy
www.malepregnancy.com

The Jackalope Conspiracy
www.sudftw.com/jackcon.htm

History of the Fisher Price Airplane
www.weathergraphics.com/tim/fisher/

Dog Island
http://thedogisland.com

California's Velcro Crop Under Challenge
http://home.inreach.com/kumbach/velcro.html

Although sites like these might be good starting points for discussing basic website credibility, the problem is that they are only starting points. Too many teachers use these sites as the beginning and end of website evaluation (along with a warning not to use Wikipedia). Not only are these sites all about making the yes/no judgment, they are also obviously fake and all about seeing through the trick. Their purpose is to shock naïve students into realizing that everything on the web is not true. That is a good lesson, but if the lesson stops there, our students will be lulled into a false sense of security, confident that the bad sites are easy to spot and easy to avoid.

If we start with these easy sites, our goal should be to increase the difficulty of the sites we expose our students to and eventually move away from the idea of website evaluation as a checklist concept, trying only to make yes/no judgments for sites. That is, making our students skeptical of the easy sites does not even achieve the intermediate goal of making them critical users, let alone the goal of encouraging them to be dialectical readers and hyperreaders.

Martin Luther King, Jr.

We might shock older students with sites like www.martinlutherking.org (which contains language not suitable for younger students). This site, a product of the white supremacist group Stormfront, is not intentionally wrong. The creators of the site likely believe what they say, and most, if not all, of the facts on the site are true. But the site is clearly biased and tries to sway readers' opinions by using a limited selection of facts to draw conclusions that are on the fringe of our map of the domain of knowledge of Martin Luther King, Jr. In a yes/no world, the answer to this site is certainly no, but it is faulty in different ways from the fake sites. Nevertheless, it raises the important topic of context and can help us understand the fringes of our domain of knowledge.

Humans are very big on hero worship. We like to build our heroes into larger than life characters. George Washington never told a lie. Paul Revere rode through the night to rouse the troops and save the burgeoning American experiment. Martin Luther King, Jr. was a saint who brought equality for all. These myths are great stories and work well for young children, but they leave us quite vulnerable. If we believe in perfection, then any taint to that perfection can bring down our whole belief system. It is well-known that Martin Luther King, Jr. had a wide range of personal issues (of course, he did; he was human). Are these the central points of his life and work, the pieces in the middle of our map of the domain of knowledge? No, but they are important for understanding the larger picture. We want to believe in the lone rider, without flaws, riding through the night to rally the troops (literally for Paul Revere, metaphorically for Martin Luther King, Jr.).

That's just not the way the world works. Lots of real human beings with real flaws have played significant roles and bit parts in history. Does this diminish the contribution of our "heroes"? Only if you believe in a myth that they must be lone riders imbued with perfection. If our goal is perfection so that we have to dismiss the flaws of individuals, we will always be disappointed. If we understand the larger domain of knowledge, the work of many people, the flaws of those people, and then put all of that in the perspective of the larger domain of knowledge, our world won't be shattered by revelations of marital infidelity (whether or not they are true). Those revelations can be placed clearly in context, probably not in the core of our domain of knowledge, but on the edge, and we can continue to value the important, good work of our heroes while recognizing their flaws.

Black Invention Myths

Now, evaluating www.martinlutherking.org is relatively easy for most of us. We can easily see that a yes/no judgment leads to a no even if some of our students can't see that. If the world were full of great sites and a few like www.martinlutherking.org, our job would be relatively easy. We could, in fact, probably get by with the yes/no judgments and simply ignore all the "bad" sites. However, the world is much more complicated and subtle. Take, for example, Black Invention Myths (www33.brinkster.com/iiiii/ inventions).

Although a few things on this site raise red flags (including a lack of information about the author), overall, the site is well done and full of a great many facts. In a world where we are on a search for facts, this might even be a good site. But the facts are only part of the story, especially the decontextualized facts, or in this case, the recontextualized facts. As we try to understand a particular invention—peanut butter or the traffic light, for example—or various inventions by black people, we need to look at the domain of knowledge from a variety of perspectives. We might look at the facts presented at this site. I have not researched all the facts in detail, but most, if not all, appear to be true. However, some of the facts are in dispute, so we might need to look at other sites with competing facts. We also might want to examine our hero-worship culture, which might lead us to think carefully about the whole concept of invention.

Again, people like to make neat and tidy packages so that individuals can be presented as heroes—George Washington Carver invented peanut butter; Elisha Graves Otis invented the elevator—as if these metaphorical lone riders rode through the night and then solely through their own hard work and inspiration produced the invention. That view ignores Albert Einstein's contention: "If I have seen further than others, it is because I was standing on the shoulders of giants." Or was that first said by Isaac Newton or John of Salisbury or an even earlier historical figure? At a minimum, invention and discovery have to do with building on the work of others. To recognize this is not to diminish the contributions of Carver or Otis or Einstein; it is to understand the reality, not the myth.

To understand the Black Invention Myths site, we have to do more than look at the facts. We have to build a fuller picture of the domain of knowledge. Otherwise, our students are in danger of lining up the site's author's facts and following the path to the same conclusions. This is tricky for our students because the point to understand is not entirely that the "facts" are in question but how the author contextualizes them to lead to conclusions. By contextualizing facts and data into a larger domain of knowledge—

and teaching our students to contextualize what they find on the web (namely put their findings into historical, verifiable, logical contexts)—we can immunize our students from accepting skewed facts as presented and following biased authors' paths to inappropriate conclusions.

I know that some of you have looked at the Black Invention Myths site and have said to yourselves that the motives of the author are clear. But many of you did not find clear motives (I know this because I have shown this site to dozens of teachers and received very mixed responses as to the author's motives). In case it is not obvious, the goal of the author is to convince you that black people are stupid. He has carefully lined up the facts to show us that black people didn't invent anything that history books say they invented.

Hopefully, those of you reading this book are smart enough not to fall for that author's line of reasoning, but the question is, How can you get your students to think critically enough so that they don't fall for what the author intends? He doesn't come out and say, "Black people are stupid," but he surely implies it. He makes a subtle argument based on facts. He supports his facts with documentation. He is not overtly biased. There are no obvious signs that this site is a bad one. There are some question marks on our checklist (such as date, but we're talking about historical inventions, so the date isn't that critical), but it's not the checklist that should lead to our concern. For many interesting sites, the checklist is ambiguous. That is why we need to help our students explore the domain of knowledge and build context for things they research. As mentioned in the beginning of this chapter, we are cognitive misers, and we won't use these skills all the time, but we need to make sure our students have these skills and practice them, so they can use them when they need to evaluate data.

Decontextualizing and Recontextualizing

Nothing lies better than facts taken out of context. Politicians do this all the time, emphasizing one vote by an opponent that might have been part of a larger bill. "My opponent is against children because he voted for a bill that took away funding medical care for children." The statement never mentions that the bill was part of making tough decisions to balance an overstretched budget or about reallocating funds from an ineffective program to a more effective one. This is the process of decontextualizing facts. They might lead you to one conclusion standing alone, but they might lead to another when given the proper context.

Now, take a series of facts out of context, picking and choosing just the right facts and putting them together to form a new context. This is the process of recontextualizing facts. Take, for example, everything that Martin Luther King, Jr. ever did that was wrong and create a website about how he was a monster, and you have www.martinlutherking.org. The facts may be right, but by decontextualizing them and recontextualizing them, they lead to the wrong conclusion.

One purpose of critical information literacy is to give our students the skills to recognize when the facts may be true but the conclusions to which a site leads are suspect.

Nazis on the Web

I once wrote an article for *Learning & Leading with Technology* magazine titled "I Read It on the Computer: It Must Be True" (Marcovitz, 1997). This article was based on a talk I had heard by Alan November about his article "Teaching Zack to Think" (1998). The premise is that a student, Zack, was faced with writing a paper about Nazism. He started a search and found the site of the American Nazi Party (that's how I remember November's talk, but the article says he went to Arthur Butz's page denying the Holocaust). The student was puzzled because his textbook spoke of Nazism as having taken place in the past. He then found the site of Yad Vashem (www.yadvashem.org), the Holocaust museum in Israel. He had a difficult time reconciling what he found in these different locations. However, by exploring one site filled with facts (true or not) and/or opinions, it is hard to build up an understanding of the domain of knowledge. In my 1997 article, I presented four sites related to Nazism. Some of the sites have come and gone, so the sites I use today (and some of these might be gone by the time you read this so you can find your own) are www.nsm88.com, www.ihr.org, www.wiesenthal.com, www.ushmm.org, and www.jdl.org.

These sites don't fill out the entire domain of knowledge, but they provide a good foundation for it. Students can work in groups to explore one site and share what they find, or they can work to explore all the sites to build the domain of knowledge. Either paper or a mind-mapping tool (such as Inspiration or bubbl.us) can be used to try to illustrate the domain of knowledge, having students attempt to figure out what ideas and sites are central to our understanding of the topic of Nazism and what ideas and sites are along the edges.

This particular topic is delicate and is not appropriate for all ages; many of you might not feel comfortable sending even high school students to a white supremacist site. But this is the basic outline of a lesson and can be adapted to a number of topics. The following section focuses on one topic that might work better for your classroom and mentions a few other topics. Additionally, I should mention that this kind of lesson could be a great opportunity for a telecollaborative project (see Chapter Four, Telecollaborative Projects) because involving people from other backgrounds can help students see different perspectives and different understandings of the domain of knowledge.

Critical Information Literacy and Climate Change

Most website evaluation is aimed at making yes/no judgments about websites. We run through our website evaluation checklist. If enough of the criteria look good, we decide a website is good. If enough do not look good, we decide it is a bad website. This becomes problematic if we are really trying to explore and understand the larger domain of knowledge around a topic.

Take, for example, climate change. Many teachers view this as settled science. They claim that the evidence is clear that human-caused climate change (sometimes referred to as AGW or anthropogenic global warming) is a fact. Although the scientific consensus seems to indicate that this is true, it is far from a simple matter. Without disagreeing with the scientific consensus, we can explore many important viewpoints on this issue. It is tempting to say that all sites that support the idea of human-caused climate change are good, and all sites that disagree with that idea are bad. Although it is true that many of the sites that disagree with the idea of human-caused climate change do not pass muster on any web evaluation checklist, we cannot discount them entirely or wipe them from a map of knowledge and viewpoints on the subject.

Here are some things to consider:

- Even if human-caused climate change is an undisputed fact in the scientific community, it is important for our understanding of the topic to understand that there are people who disagree with this thinking and why.

- Science is not black and white. The scientific inquiry process is all about keeping an open mind and questioning what we believe. The current scientific consensus is not the final word, so we need to understand the shortcomings of our current understanding and how that understanding might change in the future.

■ Even if human-caused climate change is true, the cost of correcting it compared with the cost of doing nothing is not clear. A more interesting exploration is looking at where the balance is. For example, why is no one suggesting that we stop all energy use now? The costs of that are too great. Viewing the issue as a complex interplay of social, political, ideological, and scientific ideas yields a much more interesting understanding of the situation than a simple black/white, yes/no approach to evaluating individual websites.

Each of these ideas is important to consider when exploring climate change, and the last would make an excellent interdisciplinary study. Rather than exploring a vague question, such as writing a report about climate change, or a fixed question, such as listing the contributions of carbon to climate change, imagine having students explore the balance between the risks of taking corrective measures and not taking corrective measures. A topic like this could be studied on various levels from elementary school to graduate school. Students will find some sites to be more or less valuable, but almost any site can contribute to an understanding of the social and political risks of doing something. Additionally, as an example of problem-based learning, the end result is not predetermined. There is not a right and wrong answer. Students can come up with answers that use various facts and opinions to justify their own conclusions. Students won't be judged on the answers they get but on how they justify their answers.

Following is a compilation of sites about climate change that provide a variety of perspectives. Many of the sites would be challenging for younger students, but most of the sites would be helpful for middle school or older students. A few sites are geared to younger children.

As a teacher, you could provide your students with this complete list of sites, or you could narrow it down to three or four sites from a variety of perspectives. You might have groups of students explore sites from a particular perspective to foster a discussion or debate among groups representing various viewpoints, or you might have each group's sites cover a variety of perspectives.

Pro, Con, and Neither Websites

I have divided the sites into Pro, Con, and Neither for those that support the view of human-caused climate change, those that oppose it, and those that do not fit into either category. However, this is a vast oversimplification. Some of the nuances are described in the comments following each site. You and your students will discover other sites in the process of mapping these sites on the domain of knowledge around climate change.

Pro

EPA: Climate Change

www.epa.gov/climatechange

> This site from the Environmental Protection Agency (EPA) serves as a clearinghouse on all the reports generated by the EPA, including the dangers of global warming and the economic consequences of various legislative proposals. The site contains a glossary and many links.

UNEP: Climate Change

www.unep.org/climatechange

> The United Nations Environment Programme brings an international perspective to the issue of climate change. This site reports on the United Nations' efforts to bring countries together around the issue of climate change. This raises important issues from a variety of countries that may be unequally impacted by climate change and unequally impacted by various proposed solutions to the problem.

Climate Change and Global Warming

www.toowarm.org

> This site assumes that climate change is an undisputed scientific fact: "In the coming decades, the biggest challenge we will face is global warming. It is no longer debatable: global temperatures are rising, and the Earth's climate is changing."

> It provides a variety of sensible approaches to solving the problem. What the site doesn't tell you is that it is a product of the Sierra Club and the website for the Sierra Club's Global Warming Campaign. What's wrong with the Sierra Club? Not a thing. However, it is an organization with a particular viewpoint on the environment. When researching a domain of knowledge, it is always helpful to know the biases of the contributors.

"The Pros and Cons of Global Warming Opinions"

http://voices.yahoo.com/the-pros-cons-global-warming-opinions-249218.html?cat=58

> This article presents evidence that human-caused climate change is true and gives a fairly good outline of some of the issues involved,

including attempts at international treaties, such as the Kyoto Protocols. It is interesting to note that this article is written by a freelance writer, not a scientist. Another interesting thing to note is that of the 10 citations in the article, six are from newspaper articles, and four are from other sources, including the World Health Organization's newsletters.

Advantages and Disadvantages of Global Warming

http://geography.about.com/od/globalproblemsandissues/a/advantages.htm

Another viewpoint to explore is that global warming will have both positive and negative effects. This site explores the positives and the negatives.

A Student's Guide to Global Climate Change

www.epa.gov/climatechange/kids

This is a site from the Environmental Protection Agency to teach children about climate change and what they can do to help.

Center for Climate and Energy Solutions: Kids Corner

www.pewclimate.org/global-warming-basics/kidspage.cfm

This is another site geared to children to explain climate change and help children understand what they can do about it.

"Disinformation About Global Warning"

www.csicop.org/si/show/disinformation_about_global_warming

This article from *The Skeptical Inquirer* takes aim at the "disinformation campaign" about climate change and attempts to rebut some of the points of climate-change deniers.

Con

Center on Climate and Environmental Policy

www.globalwarmingheartland.org

This site is a fairly comprehensive discussion of the view that climate change is not caused by humans. Overall, it does not take a strongly emotional view of the topic; it lays out a variety of facts and opinions refuting the idea of human-caused climate change. Its "What's New" section changes every few days and includes articles that relate to the economic costs of measures to combat climate change.

Climate Physics Institute

http://climatephysics.com

This is a very interesting site, aimed at presenting a scientific view of climate change to nonscientists. Its goal is to use scientific arguments to undercut the case for human-caused climate change. On our checklist, it loses credibility quite quickly with a clearly biased approach, introducing such terms as "Al Gore Warming (AGW)." Its clear problems (at least, clear to a thinking adult) make this an ideal site for a basic exercise in information website evaluation. Students who are attempting to make a yes/no judgment about a site should be able to dismiss this site as problematic. However, simply dismissing this site would be a significant loss. This site clearly advocates for a particular viewpoint, but it does that well and at a reading level that is accessible to many students.

Climate science—any science, really—is more than a simple matter of establishing facts and coming to a conclusion for all time. It is a matter of weighing evidence, testing hypotheses, and coming to tentative conclusions that have to be reexamined as new evidence is found. This site presents excellent evidence that is opposed to the conclusion that climate change is human caused. Currently, this evidence is overwhelmed by evidence that leads to the opposite conclusion, and the current scientific consensus leans strongly toward this opposite conclusion. However, the evidence presented at a site like this is still important. If a student comes to this site and uses only this material, that student has failed to look at the larger domain of knowledge. But if a student ignores this site because it is opposed to the conclusions of other sites, that student also has failed to explore the larger domain of knowledge.

Global Warming Hoax: Global Warming or Global Warning

www.squidoo.com/falseglobalwarming

This website takes a very political and emotional view of climate change. It refers to evidence without clearly showing evidence. It also assigns political motives to those who promote the idea of human-caused climate change. For example: "Al Gore's army is going to have to get more creative and blame any weather event whatsoever, be it hurricanes, tsunamis, or floods that have battered the planet for eons, and yes even global cooling, on their favorite justification to tax, regulate and control every aspect of our life—global warming." To an even greater degree than http://climatephysics.com, this site would not pass muster with any checklist, but it reveals an important part of the domain of knowledge. Although it takes an extreme view, it raises very important questions, such as, What kinds of regulations and government controls are necessary to lessen the impact of climate change? What kinds of expenses, through taxes, loss of productivity, and so on, will be needed? How much personal freedom will we need to give up? This site takes an extreme stance that the goal of promoters of concern for human-caused climate change, such as Al Gore, is to gain more control over our lives. We can use this site to gain insights into those extreme views and raise appropriate questions about government regulation, taxation, and control.

"White House Releases Global Warming Report"

http://usgovinfo.about.com/b/2008/05/31/white-house-releases-global-warming-report.htm

This article discusses and links to a 2008 report released by the Bush administration about the effects of global warming. Although the site seems to be unbiased, it has a decidedly anti-Bush tone and can help to raise the issue of different approaches by various presidents to this controversy. Even more interesting than the article and the report are the comments by readers. The sources of the comments lack all credibility. A website checklist would throw this in the garbage, but the issues it raises are real and important.

If you're looking for facts, ignore the readers' comments section (not because it has no facts but because it has no credibility), but if you are looking for a snapshot into some of the issues, readers' comments are powerful reminders of people's concerns about the overreaching powers of government: ("England feeling more like a police state every week that goes by—with cameras everywhere on our roads and in our streets monitoring us, fines and penalties for those who occasionally speed 5 mph over the 30 mph speed limit once in a blue moon, scaremongering on almost every topic …"); government and business propaganda ("Why should we have to pay for the banks losses in investments that didn't work out. We have no recession looming, manipulative rubbish from the banks and their controllers are creating a crisis to not only remedy their losses from buying into the sub prime market but to maintain a state of fear where we are all easier to mainipulate …"); and concern for the burden of climate change policies on the third world ("The double edged sword that third world countries face from so called global warming and the restrictions that are placed on their methods as a consequence are what may really cause the food shortages").

Are these and other issues raised by the commenters real? Are the readers' claims in the comments section full of facts? If your goal is to find the answer in the first page of Google results, then the answer is no. But if your goal is to explore the issue, this site is a great launching point. The concerns are at least real concerns to particular individuals. Viewing a government report with a skeptical eye is a good lesson for our students. If nothing else, your students can take this as a call to action to look at this issue from the perspective of citizens in third-world countries. The issues they face are different from the ones faced in the United States. Don't take the words of the site or the comments or the referenced report as the truth, but don't ignore them either. Figure out where they fit into the larger domain of knowledge about climate change.

"There Is NO Man-Made Global Warming"
www.canadafreepress.com/2004/deweese121404.htm

This is another article that is opposed to the idea of human-caused climate change. It raises allegations of money corrupting the scientific process as well as the political motives of the "radical green agenda":

> Those who have been fighting against the radical green agenda have been warning that modern-day environmentalism has little to do with protecting the environment. Rather, it is a political movement led by those who seek to control the world economies, dictate development, and redistribute the world's wealth. (para. 26, Tokyo Climate Control Protocol)

Like the previous site, it is very political and emotionally charged, but it raises some important questions as we look at the larger domain of knowledge.

"Global Warming, The Big Con"
www.americanchronicle.com/articles/view/9145

> From a checklist point of view, this 2006 article is without merit, but it approaches the debate from an angle not seen in other sites. It doesn't use the term *moral panic*, but it describes the rhetoric over climate change as if it were a moral panic, comparing those who speak about the problems of climate change to a person walking the streets with a sandwich board declaring that the world is coming to an end. By describing this issue in terms of a senseless panic, the author provides another lens through which to explore the domain of knowledge.

"Man-Made Global Warming Is Not Scientific Consensus"
www.collativelearning.com/no concensus on man-made climate change.html

> This web page raises the important question of whether the evidence is strong enough to support the proposed solutions to climate change: "There is a consensus from the world's most powerful political institutions, but that is not enough for people across the world to make the economic sacrifices that are being proposed to solve the supposed problem." This page contains a number of links to videos and articles from climate-change skeptics.

Anthropogenic Global Warming Used to Promote Socialism
www.appinsys.com/globalwarming/AGWSocialism.htm

> This is another site whose authors say that the idea of human-caused climate change is a conspiracy to promote a socialist agenda. The site's authors express the view that the United Nations, the Rockefeller Foundation, Oxfam, environmental groups, and others are spreading propaganda about the "non-science of global warming," aided by the degrowth movement, which encourages people to renounce the "uncontrolled consumerism of contemporary capitalist societies," quoting French economist Serge Latouche, one of the degrowth movement's leaders.

Friends of Science: Providing Insight into Climate Change
www.friendsofscience.org

> This is the main site of the organization Friends of Science. They claim to be made up of volunteers, many of whom are scientists and engineers

who are skeptical about human-caused climate change. They do not do any of their own research, but they compile reports that others have done. They provide links to many articles, some of which are rated by their technical difficulty.

DemandDebate

www.demanddebate.com

This site is designed for students and parents and offers a strongly biased view that climate change is not caused by humans. Like many other sites, they set up Al Gore as a straw man against a handful of scientists who do not believe in human-caused climate change without mentioning the larger number of scientists who believe in human-caused climate change.

Neither

"Thatcher becomes latest recruit in Monckton's climate sceptic campaign"

www.guardian.co.uk/environment/2010/jun/22/thatcher-climate-sceptic-monckton

This article provides a well-balanced glimpse at the politics of climate change in the British government. The author is policy and communications director at the Grantham Research Institute on Climate Change and the Environment at London School of Economics and Political Science.

"Global Warming and Social Evolution"

http://porkupineblog.blogspot.com/2007/02/global-warming-and-social-evolution.html

This blog post doesn't question whether or not climate change is caused by humans but raises some interesting theories about the social evolution of humans due to changes in climate in prehistoric times and what that might mean in the future. The blogger concludes with these interesting ideas: "One means to curtail the warming trend would be to shift to an economy that was human scale, decentralized, did not depend upon warfare—that ultimate polluter—nor a lot of wasteful long-distance carriers. This would mean the break up of that class divided, hierarchical, authoritarian structure. Put simply, state and class got us into this mess, state and class have to go so we can clean up the mess. Climate change may be the quite literal 'hot house' of our next stage of social evolution!"

Wiki: Global Warming: Government and Politics

http://peswiki.com/index.php/
Directory:Global_Warming:Government_&_Politics

This is a wiki from the Pure Energy Systems network of companies in the clean energy field. This particular wiki points to news articles and non-news sites that look at issues relating to climate change and government.

"Green This! The Ideological Divide"

http://entertainment.msn.com/green/zogby1

This article from the editor of the MSN Live Earth section discusses the varying opinions about climate change and then reports on surveys from Zogby International about what Americans believe about climate change. Although the article sets up the divide as between "rotten egg throwers" rabble-rousing against climate change and the "well-researched" supporters of climate change, it does point out that some of the arguments against climate change are more reasonable. This distinction makes this an important site because it is important for our students to understand that an idea isn't bad because many of its supporters are "rotten egg throwers" and "rabble rousers." It is important to get beyond that and look at the substance. The site also has a link to the full results of the Zogby surveys.

"Conservatives' Doubts About Global Warming Grow"

www.gallup.com/poll/126563/conservatives-doubts-global-warming-grow.aspx

This article reports on the results of a poll from Gallup about Americans' changing views on climate change. The article's bottom-line conclusions: "There has been a significant shift in Americans' views on global warming in the past two years to a position of lessened concern compared with two years ago. Global warming attitudes have become *more politically divided* over time, and while the shifts toward diminished worry are evident among all party groups, ideological liberals' views have been more stable than conservatives' or moderates' views. Given that *conservatives outnumber liberals* in the U.S. population by roughly 2 to 1, any significant change in the former group's attitudes toward global warming is enough to move the needle on global warming attitudes among all Americans."

Climate Change Skepticism

www.guardian.co.uk/environment/climate-change-scepticism

This is a constantly updated collection of news articles from *The Guardian* newspaper in London. All the articles do not focus on the United Kingdom, and the international perspective is helpful.

Other Topics

This chapter has given a wide range of resources about climate change from a variety of perspectives, although it does not represent the entire domain of knowledge around climate change. Exercise 3 at the end of this chapter lists a few other topics you might find appropriate for your classroom. You might want to explore something in the context of your curriculum, or you might want to pick a topic that is not in your curriculum and make the lesson solely about critical information literacy. For example, a look at Columbus Day might include sites like the following:

www.bbc.co.uk/schools/famouspeople/standard/columbus/index.shtml#focus

www.imahero.com/herohistory/christopher_herohistory.htm

http://library.thinkquest.org/J002678F/columbus.htm

See http://studentpersonalpages.loyola.edu/mrjones1/www/loyola/What_Can_You_Believe__Teacher.html for an elementary teacher's lesson plan using this topic. Note that the lesson is not restricted to web resources and includes background knowledge from age-appropriate books. A topic like this can help our students question the accounts of Christopher Columbus as the hero who "discovered" America and lead to an exploration of where Columbus landed, what was already known about the world being round, the people who were already here, and more.

Lesson Ideas

The Debate. Assign some groups of students sites that take a skeptical view toward human-caused climate change and other groups sites that view that climate change is real, and have them debate the issue. A structured debate with strict time limits works very well. This can be done in an hour:

- four minutes each for opening statements (8 minutes)

- a three-minute break to prepare rebuttals (3 minutes)

- five minutes each for rebuttals (10 minutes)

- a three-minute break to prepare an additional rebuttal (3 minutes)

- five minutes each for the additional rebuttal (10 minutes)

- a three-minute break to prepare closing statements (3 minutes)

- five minutes each for closing statements (10 minutes)

This is a total of 47 minutes. If your class allows additional time, you can have a 10-minute question-and-answer period from a panel of judges, possibly followed by the judges discussing and voting on the winner. The judges can be those students in the class not participating in the debate, the teacher and/or other teachers, another class (either in the room or viewing the debate via Skype or other videoconferencing), or visiting parents. Strict timekeeping by the teacher and good questions from the panel can make this a wonderful activity. The downside of this activity is that a debate fosters the yes/no divide rather than the broader understanding of the issues.

The Comprehensive Guide. Because this activity is based around websites, it is an ideal opportunity to create something, perhaps a wiki or a blog, for the web. Groups of students could study different aspects of the issue and prepare sections of a website (blogs and wikis) as a kid-friendly guide to the topic. Rather than dividing up students on a yes/no basis, groups of students can look at political questions, economic questions, opinion polling, third world countries, greenhouse gases, and health-related issues.

The Uncertainty WebQuest. This study could make an excellent WebQuest (see The Learning Power of WebQuests, http://tommarch.com/writings/wq_power.php, or http://webquest.org). Both sites contain large, open-ended topics and web resources. A WebQuest could be built around the essential question: What, if anything, should be done to prevent the problems of climate change? This realistic question can lead your students to explore the problem from a variety of perspectives, including winners vs. losers and costs vs. benefits of actions. It could be narrowed down to a task with specific parts, such as propose the one most important solution to the problem of climate change, describe who stands to benefit and who stands to lose from that solution, and justify why you think that is or is not an appropriate action to take. This technique can be tailored to a variety of grade levels, with high school students exploring the science and politics in depth and elementary school students presenting a basic understanding of some of the issues.

I leave these general ideas to you for lessons because when you are in the classroom, you are in the best position to tailor these suggestions to your students or to come up with your own ideas. Just remember that the goal of a project like this isn't to find neat and simple solutions. Instead, the interrelated goals are to lead students to think deeply about a topic, to explore the wider domain of knowledge, and to understand that, although some sites are better than others, many sites can help us understand the wide range of opinions and data on issues—whether or not we rely on them for facts.

Conclusion

Critical information literacy is not about neat and tidy outcomes or simple checklists. It is about preparing our students with the mental tools to be able to tackle the real and messy web. It is a progression of understanding that might start in first grade with very simple ideas. It can include spotting fake websites and using simple checklists, but it can't stop there. As students' cognitive abilities grow, their understandings of the messy nature of knowledge must grow. Some explorations are about facts and simple truths, but others are about the nature of fact and truth. Some explorations are about finding the good stuff and discarding the bad, but others are about learning to analyze complex shades of gray.

We want our students to be able to discard obviously wrong sites easily. We want our students to be skeptical and develop the skills of a critical reader who can make sound judgments about sites that are not obviously balanced or biased. But we want more. We want our students to be skillful navigators and skillful mappers of domains of knowledge, capable of exploring deeply a wide range of facts and opinions about a topic. We don't expect them to do this every time, and we don't expect them to learn these skills in one quick and easy lesson. Over time, using many different examples, we need to teach students evaluative skills, so that whenever they need to make judgments about what they find on the web, they can call upon these skills to think deeply.

Exercises

1. Often in school, or through various media, we learn shorthand statements that capture some aspects of the truth, yet they fall short in other ways, In most cases, if we understood why these statements fell short, we would have a much deeper understanding of the knowledge domain in question and would likely find the topic itself more interesting. For example, we learn that "in 1492, Columbus sailed the ocean blue" and that he discovered America. But what did he really discover? And in what sense did he discover it? Choose one of the following commonplace statements (or come up with a similar commonly accepted "fact"). Then use the web to see what you can learn about why it may be limited or false in some interesting way. If you already know a lot about the domain, keep searching until you come up with something you didn't already know. Can you trust what you've found on the web?

    - Columbus discovered America in 1492.

    - You should choose your food from the four food groups.

    - There are five senses: taste, smell, touch, sight, and hearing.

    - There are seven continents.

    - People in France speak French.

    - There are eight planets in our solar system.

    - Milk is the best treatment for an ulcer.

    - Benjamin Franklin discovered electricity.

    - In the United States, slavery was confined to the south.

    Source: This exercise is adapted from "How can we learn to read critically?" (www.cii.illinois.edu/InquiryPage/bin/u10324.html), created by Bertram (Chip) Bruce. It is used here with permission and is based on the ideas in his article (Bruce, 2000).

2. Alternatively, pick one of the three lesson ideas in this chapter (debate, comprehensive guide, uncertainty WebQuest) or come up with your own and create an assignment for your students that requires them to explore climate change and the variety of perspectives on the subject.

3. Find another topic that is age-appropriate for your students and create an assignment that asks them to explore that topic and the variety of perspectives on the subject. Some sample topics might include school uniforms, childhood vaccines, the role of money in politics, physical education and/or recess in schools, vending machines in schools, Columbus Day, the value of chemicals (such as sodium hexametaphosphate) in our food, or the authorship of Shakespeare's works. These are simply examples to get you thinking.

References

Beck, S. (1997). The good, the bad & the ugly: Or, why it's a good idea to evaluate web sources. Retrieved January 23, 2012, from http://lib.nmsu.edu/instruction/eval.html

Bruce, B. C. (2000, February). Credibility of the web: Why we need dialectical reading. *Journal of Philosophy of Education, 34*(1), 97–109, retrieved January 22, 2012, from http://www.ideals.illinois.edu/bitstream/handle/2142/13425/credibility.pdf

Burbules, N. C., & Callister, T. A., Jr. (2000). *Watch IT: The risks and promises of information technologies for education.* Boulder, CO: Westview Press.

Fiske, S. T., & Taylor, S. E. (1991). *Social cognition* (2nd ed.). New York, NY: McGraw-Hill.

Kaufmann, W. (1977). The art of reading. In W. Kaufmann, *The future of the humanities* (pp. 47–83). New York, NY: Thomas Y. Crowell.

Marcovitz, D. (1997, November). I read it on the computer: It must be true. *Learning & Leading with Technology, 25*(3), 18–21.

November, A. (1998). Teaching Zack to think. *High School Principal, 78*(1), 5. Retrieved January 24, 2012, from http://novemberlearning.com/resources/archive-of-articles/teaching-zack-to-think

CHAPTER THREE

The Overhyped Dangers of Wikipedia

My daughter came home from school the other day and said she lost credit in her language arts class because she couldn't find any information about the song she was researching. She was researching a song to compare its themes to those found in Dickens' *A Tale of Two Cities*. The song she was researching was "Oxford Town" by Bob Dylan. A quick Google search (in December, 2010), indeed, produced very little on this song beyond the actual lyrics and a Wikipedia article about the album on which it appeared with only one sentence about the song itself. Refining the search to add the word *meaning* brings up a couple of sites that seemed promising, such as www. songmeanings.net and http://lyricsmeaning.davidsmit.za.net, but these sites are merely forums for fans to discuss what they think the lyrics might mean. The second site has no comments; the first actually has some useful information along with several unhelpful comments. It is interesting that this collection of comments might be considered better simply because it is not Wikipedia.

So, what is a girl to do? She is faced with a challenge to find information about a topic, and she knows next to nothing about it. She hears the voice of the Wikipedia police in her head and tells me, "I don't like Wikipedia, and neither does my teacher." In fact, Wikipedia was only slightly helpful to her. As I was first writing this chapter, the Wikipedia article about the song consisted of only three sentences:

> "Oxford Town" is a song written by Bob Dylan in 1962. It was first recorded in Columbia's Studio A on 6 December 1962 for his second album, *The Freewheelin' Bob Dylan*. It treats the case of James Meredith, the first "negro" student at the University of Mississippi in Oxford, Mississippi, who was enrolled on October 1, 1962. (http://en.wikipedia.org/wiki/Oxford_Town retrieved December 6, 2010)

And it's Wikipedia, so we can't even be sure it is accurate, right? Let's start with a simpler question than understanding the meaning of the song. On what album did "Oxford Town" appear? Let's raise the stakes. Your friend is on a game show and is using you as a lifeline to answer this question, which is worth $1 million. You do a quick search and up comes this Wikipedia article. Are you sure? Are you $1 million sure? For me the answer is that I am pretty sure but not $1 million sure. However, now that I have a really good idea of the answer, it is easy to verify on many other sites (e.g., www.bobdylan.com or a quick search of the iTunes store), where you'll be able to see (and possibly listen to) the album and the songs on it.

Trust But Verify

This simple exercise of verification can be extended beyond basic facts. The 2010 article is limited, but it gives us a starting point for our search. We can easily verify that the University of Mississippi is in Oxford, Mississippi. We can easily verify that James Meredith was the first "negro" student there in October 1962. Would I bet my life or $1 million that these facts are accurate? Of course not, but I don't have to. I can verify these facts and more in print and nonprint sources. This is true for Wikipedia, and it is true for any other source. Granted, we might have more confidence in other sources because they meet standards on our checklist (e.g., named authors with credentials), but if we are not using Wikipedia as the final word but as a starting point, it is an excellent tool to begin a search.

> However, Wikipedia deserves the same place in most modern assign-ments that the *Encyclopedia Britannica* did in most of ours. It was a starting point with a collection of additional references for our research. It gave us the general background we needed to dig further. Wikipedia does the same with remarkable reliability, given the success of the crowdsourcing model. Wikipedia, however, makes most of those primary sources and deeper research possibilities available within just a few clicks. We don't need to teach our kids not to use Wikipedia. We need to teach them to make those extra few clicks and decide for themselves whether the Wikipedia entry has merit. It's a skill that is broadly applicable in an age of information overload and Google's billions of search results. (Dawson, 2010, para. 9)

In 2005, Wikipedia was quickly becoming a very popular source of information. The journal *Nature* did a study comparing the accuracy of articles about scientific topics in Wikipedia and *Encyclopedia Britannica* (Giles, 2005). Reviewers of the articles found the same number of serious errors in each source and slightly more minor errors in Wikipedia than in *Encyclopedia Britannica*. The largest downside they found was that the Wikipedia articles tended to be written more poorly.

Would you trust a source that had four serious errors and 123 minor errors in just 42 articles? Would you bet $1 million that the information is accurate? I hear you saying "no." Then why would you ever trust *Encyclopedia Britannica*? Wikipedia is no better, but they are both great starting points to get the basic, albeit unverified, facts. In most cases, either of the sources is the beginning of a search, not the end.

The problem is not that students are using Wikipedia. "What's wrong is ending one's research there too, which is what many teachers fear their students are doing" (Bennington, 2008). A first step in critical information literacy is to understand that any given source is fallible. At a minimum, students should click on links to the sources listed in a Wikipedia article to see the original (sometimes primary source) information. Additionally, students should verify the information they find in Wikipedia (or any other source) by confirming it with other sources. Finally, students should try to understand the larger domain of knowledge (see Chapter Two) to understand where the content of the Wikipedia article might be lacking or biased (see, for example, Moran, 2010).

Student-Certified Wikipedia Articles

In 2005, Andy Carvin wrote a blog post titled "Turning Wikipedia into an Asset for Schools" (Carvin, 2005). He suggested that Wikipedia is a powerful tool, not as a source of information but as fodder for verification. He suggested that classrooms across the country should research the content of Wikipedia articles and verify their accuracy. Those that turn out to be inaccurate can be corrected, and those that turn out to be accurate can receive a certification that students have verified them. This idea introduces a different relationship with information: information is not to be trusted without verification. It is easy to find a piece of information, hope that it is correct, and rewrite it in your own words. But this is not information literacy. Taking this to the next step to think about the information and then finding out its shortcomings is what we want our students to be able to do.

"Oxford Town" in the End

Simply relying on the first things that came up on a search engine and ignoring user-generated content led to a blank paper for my daughter. She needed to get started somewhere, and Wikipedia was not only as good a place to start as anything, it was better than anything (or, in this case, nothing). Knowing a few basic facts allowed her to dig deeper, verify those facts, and find many more. My hope is that when she is done with this project, she will post it online. Where will she post it? Wikipedia, of course. (See Box 3.1, Wikipedia is Constantly Changing, to get a sense of the site's changeability.)

Box 3.1

Wikipedia is Constantly Changing

Here is the third (and final) sentence from the December 2010 Wikipedia entry on "Oxford Town":

> It [Dylan's song] treats the case of James Meredith, the first 'negro' student at the University of Mississippi in Oxford, Mississippi.

Compare that with the third sentence in the January 2012 Wikipedia page (a page that was last modified in October 2011):

> The song was composed in response to an open invitation from *Broadside* magazine for songs about one of the top news events of 1962: the enrollment of a black student, James Meredith, in the University of Mississippi on October 1.

The newer entry is more informative. But the changes don't stop there. Four more paragraphs have been added, as have notes, references, and links.

Exercises

1. Find an entry in Wikipedia about which you know something and edit it. This can be a small or large change. The purpose of this activity is to see how easy it is to edit. Note that many Wikipedia entries are now locked from changing so be sure to find one that is not locked.

2. Go to a Wikipedia entry and read the history and the discussion. Try to identify if a single user is acting as a de facto editor for that entry by making many corrections and possibly reversing several inappropriate changes.

3. Find a Wikipedia entry and verify that it is accurate. Follow its references, and look for references that are not included. If you find something incomplete or inaccurate, edit the entry.

References

Bennington, A. (August, 2008). Dissecting the web through Wikipedia. *American Libraries, 39*(7), 46–48.

Carvin, A. (2005, July 11). Turning Wikipedia into an asset for schools [Blog post]. Retrieved from http://www.andycarvin.com/?p=738

Dawson, C. (2010, November 4). Teachers: Please stop prohibiting the use of Wikipedia, in ZDNet Education [Blog post]. Retrieved from http://www.zdnet.com/blog/education/teachers-please-stop-prohibiting-the-use-of-wikipedia/4319

Giles, J. (2005, December 15). Internet encyclopaedias go head to head. *Nature, 438,* 900–901.

Moran, M. (2010, March 20). Top ten reasons students cannot cite or rely on Wikipedia. In *Finding Dulcinea* [Website]. Retrieved December 6, 2010, from http://www.findingdulcinea.com/news/education/2010/march/The-Top-10-Reasons-Students-Cannot-Cite-or-Rely-on-Wikipedia.html

Oxford Town. (2010, December 6). In Wikipedia. Retrieved December 6, 2010, from http://en.wikipedia.org/wiki/Oxford_Town

Oxford Town. (2012, January 24). In Wikipedia. Retrieved January 24, 2012, from http://en.wikipedia.org/wiki/Oxford_Town

CHAPTER FOUR

Telecollaborative Projects

Telecollaborative projects are projects where more than one classroom uses technology to connect. The goal of telecollaborative projects is to expand the walls of the classroom, often to share data or perspectives with different people.

Many telecollaborative projects involve doing something you are already doing and then connecting to others to make it better. For example, a classroom might choose to plant butterfly bushes to attract and observe monarch butterflies. This requires no communication technology. The problem is that the butterflies seem to appear from nowhere. They simply flutter across the field, and there they are. But where did they come from? Certainly, you can read about the overwintering sites in Mexico and butterflies' journeys to sites across North America and back again. But imagine communicating with people from around North America who are also watching for the monarch butterflies through the Journey North project (www.learner.org/jnorth/monarch). Now the abstract idea of migration becomes real, as your students read reports of butterfly sightings and follow the journey of the butterflies on maps, anticipating their arrival in your school.

Does your classroom study weather? Most children have no idea of weather patterns. Weather seems to appear magically out of nowhere. Perceiving weather conditions in other parts of the United States and the world can be a difficult concept for children. Because they live in the here and now, children assume that the weather in their area is the same as everywhere else.

Over the years, many projects have worked to solve this problem by having classrooms from different climatic zones share weather data and discuss the weather from a wider perspective. This can be as simple as posting current weather conditions on a daily or weekly basis or as complex as a detailed study of the weather with multiple classrooms. For an even more complex study of weather, you might look into projects like The Globe Program (www.globe.gov), which involves classrooms from around the world collecting data with strict scientific protocols and interacting with the data collected and scientists who are using the data to study such things as climate change. A site that's designed for younger students is Weather Watch: An Interactive Weather Project. To learn more about this project and how to register your class, see the site (www.cyberbee.com/weatherwatch/participation.html).

How big is the earth? You can certainly look up the information, but with a little help from other schools and The Noon Day Project (www.k12science.org/curriculum/noonday/), you can use a trick that Eratosthenes used over 2000 years ago to measure it yourself. You just need to measure the shadow cast by a meter stick and compare that to the shadows measured at several places around the world.

These projects involve observations of the natural world. They benefit from telecollaboration because your class can make observations and collect data only in your area. Connecting with others allows you to use real data from other areas. Sometimes geography isn't the problem as much as perspective. Peters (2009) says, "We only realize how deeply enveloped we are in our own culture when we have an opportunity to stand outside of it and look at it from a stranger's perspective" (p. 4). As hard as it is for students to understand that the weather might be different in different areas, it is even harder for them to understand that different people think and live in different ways from their own. Connections can be made in simple or complex ways.

Several years ago, I talked to a teacher who taught in a private school with a population of mostly middle- to upper-class white children. They went to a play in Baltimore that dealt with issues of race. Meanwhile, another class from the inner city, mainly socioeconomically disadvantaged African-American students, also watched the play. Needless to say, they had different perspectives about the play. The power of telecollaboration became apparent when the two classes connected and began an online discussion of the play. Although it's easy for a teacher to bring up different perspectives with students, the message is much more powerful when it comes from an exchange with peers.

Classrooms by themselves are missing many things. These might include racial diversity, socioeconomic diversity, cultural diversity, adult involvement, access to different geographic regions, foreign perspectives, students who speak languages other than English, and more. Not every classroom lacks all of these things, but even the best classrooms lack some of them. No classroom, for example, is in two different places at the same time. For a great deal of what happens in a classroom, these missing pieces aren't necessary. However, sometimes there are things we might want to do if we could be in two places at once. Telecollaborative projects can give our classrooms that access. We can't take a trip across the country to follow the migratory patterns of robins, but we can connect with other classrooms in other places to track them through the Journey North's American Robin Migration Tracking Project

■ CONTRARIAN PERSPECTIVES

"What's shrinking is the American view of the world: We are unable to speak foreign languages, unwilling to read foreign news, and unequipped to understand foreign cultures. We naturally perceive other cultures the easy way: by watching them on TV or glimpsing them through a porthole of the Internet. This conveys images, not understanding. Rather than shrinking our globe, this shallow electronic information system makes foreign cultures more distant." (Stoll, 1999, p. 118) (www.learner.org/jnorth/robin). We can't visit grocery stores around the country or around the world to collect data on price differences, to understand differing economic conditions, and to use real-world data to learn math concepts, but we can connect to classrooms collecting the same data we are collecting in different places through the Global Grocery List Project (http://landmark-project.com/ggl). We can't truly experience other cultures, but we can have our students truly connect with people from other cultures through ePals' The Way We Are Classroom Project (www.epals.com/projects/info.aspx?DivID=TheWayWeAre_overview).

The power of telecollaborative projects is to transcend the natural barriers of being confined in space to learn in ways that we can't by sitting in our own classrooms. Telecollaborative projects don't solve every educational problem, and they can't always replace being someplace else. We can't fool ourselves that an email exchange gives us a perfect picture of a culture, comparable to living abroad over an extended period of time, but it is a start to help us "avoid the marginalization of minority cultures by reaching beyond food festivals and Flag Day celebrations and spending more thought on how to deeply integrate global perspectives into the curriculum" (Peters, 2009, p. 4).

Activity Structures

Judi Harris (1998*a* & 1998*b*) and (2010) categorizes different types of activity structures for telecollaborative projects. She argues that lesson plans are of limited use because teachers have to adapt them to their own situations. Instead, she believes that activity structures provide a framework for types of lessons that can be developed for a wide range of situations. She divides telecollaborative activity structures into four main categories: interpersonal exchanges, information exchanges, work and experiences exchanges, and strategies exchanges. Each of these categories consists of several potential activity structures. Being able to categorize what you do into a specific activity structure is not important, but thinking about activity structures helps you understand the range of possibilities of how telecollaborative projects can help your classroom. The rest of this section describes a wide range of activity structures and gives several examples. For more examples, visit the Texas Technology Integration Professional Development Corps' website (http://txtipd.wm.edu), which bases its program on Harris's research.

Interpersonal Exchanges

Interpersonal exchanges include a range of activities when students and/or adults are exchanging information. The most common activity structure in this category is the keypal structure, where individual students exchange emails with one another. This exchange could take the form of a cultural exchange, a discussion around a topic, or creative writing. The K–12 social learning network called ePals (www.epals.com) can help facilitate exchanges like this with its platform for safe, monitored email and its suggested lesson plans for exchanges. While we can imagine sending off a letter or email and hoping to get one back, ePals projects take this a step further by outlining a series of emails tied to objectives and assessments that form the basis of a thought-provoking lesson plan.

For example, ePals' The Way We Are project (www.epals.com/projects/info.aspx?DivID= TheWayWeAre_overview) asks three essential questions: How is my life similar to and different from my ePal's life? How does the natural environment where my ePal lives affect his or her life? and What effect does the culture in my ePal's region have on his or her life?

The questions are answered via a series of five email exchanges with specific guidelines, and the project culminates by having students "create final digital presentations about themselves and their ePals reflecting an increased understanding of the differences and commonalities between their cultures, their environments and their lives." ePals provides the infrastructure and the collaborative model for each project, but the projects run by making connections with other teachers—ePals provides a mechanism for making these connections—so two teachers can modify the ways they interact however they see fit.

Keypal projects can be quite effective, although they provide some logistical challenges. Global classrooms eliminate one-on-one communication and allow entire classes to communicate with one another as they study a common topic. This could be as simple as reading a common text and using a discussion board to open the discussion to more than one classroom. This can be done through individual postings or designated class respondents, where one student (or the teacher) summarizes the discussion to post to the common discussion board. Remember that all of this adds value if it provides something you are lacking in your own classroom. Imagine, for example, the different kinds of discussions that might take place around race while discussing Mark Twain's *The Adventures of Huckleberry Finn* (1884) in northern or southern U.S. classrooms with populations of different races. In those cases, the global classroom helps to bring a different perspective to the conversation. A global classroom might involve something as simple as the Our Footprints, Our Future project (http://media.iearn.org/node/733), which asks students to calculate their carbon footprints and post their information on the discussion board.

With the advent of easy and cheap videoconferencing (see, e.g., Skype—www.skype.com), electronic appearances are easy to do. This is nothing more than bringing in a guest speaker to your class electronically. It can also be done asynchronously with email exchanges, discussion boards, or blogs. Impersonations can be another related activity structure, in which the guest might be a character from a book or a person from history. This can use any of the communication tools discussed, or it might take place via social media, such as Twitter (http://twitter.com) or Facebook (www.facebook.com). More extended relationships with outside experts are referred to as telementoring. This could take the form of one-on-one mentoring through a program like the Association for Women in Mathematics Mentor Network (http://sites.google.com/site/awmmath/programs/mentor-network), or it could be in the form of group mentoring, possibly arranging for an outside expert to assist a group of students with a large project. The Electronic Emissary project (http://emissary.wm.edu) is designed to help connect K–12 classrooms with mentors willing to share their expertise in various knowledge and skill areas.

Information Exchanges

Information exchange activities help target the lack of information and data available in one classroom. This could be an activity used to gather more data than one classroom could, or it could be used to gather data from different geographical areas that differ from your area. These activities might involve information sharing between two or more classrooms; information comparison/contrast, in which the data from different areas is compared; information building/organization, in which the data is stored and organized; and data pooling/analysis, in which the data is not only shared and organized but also analyzed.

Information exchanges can include simple activities, such as the Oreo Project (www.jenuinetech.com/Projects/2011oreo/2011ohome.html), in which students stack Oreo cookies to see how high they stack and provide data for graphing and analysis. The Human Genetics Project (www.k12science.org/curriculum/genproj/) asks whether the dominant trait is most common. Rather than one classroom collecting a few examples and trying to base conclusions on a small sample, this project pools data from many classrooms to explore this genetic question.

Another simple example is Seasonal Changes Through Our Eyes and Yours, which connects classrooms in various geographic regions by having elementary school classes compare their observations to observations from other regions (www.lakelandschools.us/do/lbrandon/Seasons/home.htm):

> Take a tree, some sun, the seasons, and the temperature. Mix in the use of technology and extension activities. Add a roomful of smiles with a fun kind of learning and you've got the perfect recipe for a successful and motivating project in which students collect and share information with another class about their environment.

The RoadKill project (http://roadkill.edutel.com) asked students to observe animals that were killed by cars between their home and school. The project, designed to involve students and teachers with scientific monitoring of an environmental parameter, used the Internet to increase participant awareness of motor vehicle hazards with wildlife.

The RoadKill project collected a larger variety and quantity of data than students in an individual classroom could gather. The project did not specify what classrooms did with the pooled data that was collected but recommended it be used as interesting data to teach mathematical principles and graphing and to teach ecological concepts. Students used the data to test hypotheses, such as whether the number of road kills increased or decreased when the moon was full. You can listen to an interview with Dr. Splatt (Brewster Bartlett), the founder of the project, and some teachers who participated in the project in the EdTechTalk Making Connections podcast at www.edtechtalk.com/node/3035.

Seasonal Changes is a simple project run by a teacher. The RoadKill project was also run by a teacher, beginning in 1993; its website has useful links to many resources. Information exchanges can also be more complex projects, like the Journey North Project (www.learner.org/jnorth), which follows the migratory patterns of various species, such as monarch butterflies, gray whales, the American robin, and the whooping crane. The professionally run Journey North project involves a wide network of classrooms that submit observations. The project includes a teacher's manual and sends out weekly newsletters for each species observed. The newsletters include updates and analyses from classrooms, as well as challenge questions to help guide class discussions.

An even more intense project is the GLOBE Program—Global Learning and Observation to Benefit the Environment (http://globe.gov). GLOBE is a network of K–12 students, teachers, and scientists from around the world who work together to help everyone learn more about our environment. Classrooms collect data, such as weather and stream acidity data, using detailed scientific protocols. Scientists use the data to monitor environmental conditions. The data, as well as some analysis and data visualizations, are shared with participating classrooms so they can perform their own scientific analyses. Because of the need for scientific accuracy, this project requires a significant commitment from participating classrooms. Teachers must attend a teacher training workshop before their classes may participate in this project. Observations are required on a regular schedule (e.g., seven days per week at solar noon for weather data), which pose logistical challenges for students and teachers.

Work and Experiences Exchanges

Work and experiences exchanges involve virtual displays and exchanges of information but do not generally entail interaction among students. That is, students simply place their information online for others to see, such as various forms of electronic publishing and telefieldtrips. Electronic publishing projects are mechanisms for creating an authentic audience for student work. Individual teachers can create sites (or blogs or wikis) to post student projects. Sites can also be shared among a few classrooms in a school, a district, or around the world.

Sometimes work and experiences exchanges can become larger efforts, often around a theme. Examples of these kinds of projects include Global Dreamers' A Piece for Peace Project (www.globaldreamers.org/10peace), an ongoing project in which students and/or classrooms are encouraged to create short videos about peace, and the iEARN project A Vision (https://media.iearn.org/projects/avision), "an anthology of students' writings on various literary genres—essays, stories, poems, and poetical sketches, which aims to showcase the youth's thoughts, viewpoints and insights of the things around them and even across borders, regardless of cultural and racial diversity." When publishing your students' work online, be careful to get parental permission, and follow your school's or school district's guidelines for making student work available online.

It is difficult to argue that a telefieldtrip is better than a real field trip, but telefieldtrips offer the opportunity to do things that can't be done any other way. Real field trips require time and money that might be in short supply, so you might visit places nearby or in another state that you cannot afford to go to, such as the Exploratorium, museum of science, art, and human perception, in San Francisco (www.exploratorium.edu) or the elephant exhibit at the Smithsonian National Zoological Park (http://nationalzoo.si.edu/Animals/AsianElephants).

And some telefieldtrips take us to places we aren't likely to visit in person. The Jason Project (www.jason.org) has been traveling to the tops of trees in rainforests and the bottoms of oceans for more than 20 years. Teams of scientists travel to places where you couldn't possibly take your students (are your students even allowed to climb a tree in the schoolyard?), send back reports, and answer questions. Jason is a well-funded and well-organized project that provides a great deal of curricular material (on forces and motion, geology, energy, ecology, and weather) to help teachers incorporate the project into their classrooms.

Though we aren't equipped to create the Jason Project on our own, many of us can use inexpensive technology to create our own telefieldtrips. Just pull out your camera, and take it with you to the museum or zoo or grocery store. Or combine this activity structure with another, and have your students take cameras on a real field trip to exchange field-trip experiences with another class that went somewhere else or with one that couldn't go at all.

Internet as Audience for Writers

In May 2010, Will Richardson wrote a provocative piece in his blog, Weblogg-ed, about his son being too nervous to publish some of his own writing on a fan fiction site (see an excerpt from his blog later in this section). Richardson raises the question: Do students ever get nervous about writing for school? Although I don't agree with his implication that the answer to this question is always no, he raises the point that it is healthy to raise the stakes in a way that encourages students to care about their writing. One way to do this is to provide an authentic audience.

A fan fiction site, like the one that Richardson mentions, is a great way to tap into an existing audience with common interests, but that won't always meet your students' needs. The easiest mechanism is simply to publish the work on your blog, wiki, or website. The problem with this is that you have to build your own audience. You can start by advertising with parents, so the parents are reading it, but that is not quite the authentic audience that will make your students care about their writing.

Another avenue for publishing is to find existing online magazines for children. For example, you can join the project A Vision, offered through iEARN (www.iearn.org/avision). This is a literary magazine produced by students for students: "Students from various countries share their thoughts and dreams, their hopes and fears, with the purpose to create a world of mutual understanding, respect, tolerance, and peace."

Alternatively, you can easily create your own literary magazine or blog. Your students can collect submissions from around your school, your district, your country, or the world and publish them online. By using blogging tools, you can collect comments from readers. If you are concerned about inappropriate comments, simply use the settings on the blog tool to moderate the comments, and you can approve them before they go online.

Another option is to create audiences by establishing an electronic pen-pal relationship with other classrooms. Taking advantage of the network established by ePals (http://epals.com), you can build your own project based on what you want your students to write about, or you can tap into an existing project around a predefined theme, such as The Way We Are Classroom Project (www.epals.com/projects/info.aspx?DivID=TheWayWeAre_overview): "Through email exchanges, students will build friendships and learn about the daily lives and characteristics of the local environment of students who live in another region of the world."

Here is an excerpt from Will Richardson's blog on Weblogg-ed (http://weblogg-ed.com/2010/nervous-writing-well-trained-teachers); he wrote about his son Tucker's reticence about sharing his writing:

> I often show FanFiction.net in my presentations as an example of passionate participation. I happen to know a couple of kids (here's one: www.fanfiction.net/s/5277860/1/The_Stag_and_the_Doe) who do fanfic on a fairly regular basis, and every now and then I check in and dig around for some good stuff to read. It's usually not too hard to find. Anyway, Tucker has been checking out the Percy Jackson stories [e.g., www.fanfiction.net/book/Percy_Jackson_and_the_Olympians] fairly regularly since after the fifth time through the series, I think the books are finally starting to lose their luster. Some of the Fanfic stories he likes more than others, but the cool thing is that he's been thinking of trying his hand at writing something himself. But at almost 11, he's still a little nervous about putting something up there for everyone to see, regardless of his own anonymity in the process.
>
> Last week when I told this story, a tech director raised her hand and said, "You know, I think it's interesting that your son is nervous about sharing his writing. Does he ever get nervous about his writing for school?" I thought for a second and said, "Um, no … you know you're right. He hardly thinks twice about that stuff." She said, "I'm guessing he'd be more motivated to work on his Percy Jackson story to make it good than he is his homework." And ever since I've been wondering why we can't instill a healthy nervousness every now and then into our writing process, now that we have these ready-made audiences (or at least easily found audiences). All it would take is a willingness on our parts to let kids write about the things they truly love from time to time and connect that to an audience larger than the classroom. Shouldn't be too hard these days.

Strategies Exchanges

The final category of activity structures listed by Harris (2010) is strategies exchanges; students collaborate in some way to solve simple or complex problems, often sharing and discussing problem-solving strategies. This might include simple information searches, in which students use clues provided by others to solve a problem. Other types of exchanges involve parallel problem solving—groups of students individually solve problems and then share solutions and strategies; joint problem solving—students from different places work together to solve a common problem; serial creating—students build on each others work; peer feedback—students critique each other's work and/or problem-solving strategies; and simulation—students role-play to solve problems. Note that many of these activities can be done within a classroom, as groups of students work together in problem-solving activities and then share their results with the rest of the class. As a teacher, you will have to decide if the benefits of bringing in other classrooms outweigh the logistical issues involved.

Simple examples of strategies exchanges are the Landmark Game (www.kidlink.org/kidspace/start.php?HoldNode=1430); schools create clues for landmarks near them or solve other classrooms' clues. And the Global SchoolNet Foundation's Geo Game (www.globalschoolnet.org/GSH/project/gg); classrooms create clues about their city.

Two teachers developed The Flat Classroom Project (www.flatclassroomproject.org) around the themes in Thomas Friedman's book *The World Is Flat*. They wanted to demonstrate to their students the power of our flat world, where the Internet has made geography less important. We no longer need our accountants, call centers, web designers, or manufacturing facilities to be right around the corner because we can communicate everything we need to do electronically (Friedman, 2007). The Flat Classroom Project demonstrates this to students by having them use Web 2.0 tools to collaborate on major projects with groups of students around the world and outsourcing part of the project to other students. The project has grown from two classrooms to dozens. The project's elements include a "deeper understanding of the effects of technology on our world that lead students to not only study but actually experience the 'flatteners'"; "students are grouped with global partners to explain trends, give personal viewpoints and create a video containing an outsourced video segment"; and the "use of an educational networking platform (e.g., Ning), blogging, posting photos, videos etc. and a collaborative environment (e.g., wiki), to connect, collaborate and create"; and "assessment based on a common criterion based rubric" (www.flatclassroomproject.org/About). The project concludes with a student summit using Elluminate (www.elluminate.com, *see also* http://support.blackboardcollaborate.com/ics/support/default.asp?deptID=8336&task=knowledge&questionID=1279) to share the work that the various groups have done.

Anne Mirtschin, a teacher in Victoria, Australia, who participated in the Flat Classroom Project, describes how it works:

> Each group is given a topic which is related to the current and future use of the Internet, usually in education. Student groups build wiki pages together, using the discussion tab to work together in asynchronous time. At the end of the 10–12 week program, students complete a video that is uploaded onto the Ning and embedded in the wiki for judging by global judges. Part of this video will include an outsourced video clip by another student in another country. (http://murcha.wordpress.com/2009/06/07/the-flat-classroom-projects-from-a-paricipants-point-of-view)

So much of what happens in schools ignores what happens in the real world (sometimes that's good and sometimes not). The Flat Classroom Project is a powerful way for students to live the communication and collaboration paradigm that is taking over in a flat world.

Peer feedback activities can take the form of peer editing and evaluation (expanding what you might do in the classroom to get the feedback from others) for creative writing, videos, or content-related writing (such as science booklets). The Digital Storytelling Classroom Project (www.epals.com/projects/info.aspx?DivID=Digital_overview) combines peer feedback with electronic publishing by connecting students with electronic partners to get feedback on their digital stories in order to prepare them for publication. Feedback might also take the form of online debates. The Web-based Inquiry Science Environment (WISE—http://wise.berkeley.edu), supported by the National Science Foundation, provides opportunities for students to explore controversial science topics, such as genetically modified food (see http://wise.berkeley.edu/teacher/projects/projectInfo.php?id=4765—you need a WISE account to view this, but you can create one for free), and to debate them with other students. Peer feedback can also take the form of exchanges where students write directions for other students to follow, such as the Monster Exchange Project (www.monsterexchange.org); students draw monsters, write instructions for others to draw the same monsters, and then exchange pictures of their creations. Parallel problem-solving activities are similar to peer feedback, but in this case, the feedback relates to the solutions to problems. Christina Lassalle, a second grade teacher at Van Bokkelen Elementary School in Severen, Maryland, writes about her participation in the Monster Exchange Project (see Box 4.1).

Simulations give students the opportunity to role-play in order to make real decisions. One of the oldest examples of this is done within the classroom with the Decisions, Decisions software from Tom Snyder Productions.

Box 4.1

Monster Exchange
Christina Lassalle

The writing objective was to write a set of directions. This objective is part of the Maryland Third Grade Language Arts Curriculum as well as the writing guide for Anne Arundel County. In the past I have had my scholars create designs using tangrams or pattern blocks to make them authentic and real life. But this project surpassed what I had done before. Scholars had to think critically when writing directions. When they read the monster descriptions of the paired school and had to follow them, they were able to critique their own directions, and from there, make their directions the best they could be. They learned that information can be perceived differently and that it is so important to be clear and precise in what you do. This experience taught more than just writing a set of directions. They learned that through communication in a telecollaborative project, the simplest of words can be perceived differently.

One thing that didn't work so well was finding the extra time to get in the computer lab to tie up loose ends. It was also an undertaking for me to make the time to upload the images to the page. The teacher I was paired up with was very patient, and I felt as though I may have been keeping her waiting. I will certainly participate in this project next year because of how valuable and authentic it was for my scholars.

In Decisions, Decisions, the software guides students, who are playing various roles, through a series of decisions and their consequences. Role-playing simulations now can extend beyond an individual classroom with such activities as The Stock Market Game (www.stockmarketgame.org), in which students make investing decisions in competition with other students.

Not everything you want to do in your classroom is right for a telecollaborative project. The positive potential is great, but there are downsides as well. It is best to start small with activities that can benefit from alternative perspectives and expanded opportunities for gathering data. Once you have a handle on the time commitments and logistical efforts, you can work to expand what you do either by joining more sophisticated projects or creating your own. Next, let's discuss some of the pitfalls of telecollaborative projects.

Pitfalls

A few years ago, I contacted several teachers who were involved with telecollaborative projects to get a behind-the-scenes view of the positives and negatives (Marcovitz, 1999). I surveyed participants in three projects and asked them about their experiences. Two of the three projects are no longer active (World Weather Watch and Signs of Autumn, Signs of Spring). The third project, The GLOBE Program (www.globe.gov) still exists. I communicated with 77 teachers about their experiences. Many of them had wonderful experiences, and many ran into several pitfalls, which I categorized as time and management, technology, curriculum, communication, and other.

Time and Management

Time and management problems were the most commonly reported problems. These include problems of not having enough time for the project, not having the appropriate time for the project (e.g., daily or regular temperature readings needing to be taken at a certain time that did not coincide with class time), and general issues of managing students as they did the project.

Both World Weather Watch and GLOBE required readings to be taken at specific times (temperatures at solar noon, for example) or on specific days of the week. In addition, GLOBE weather readings were required every day, including weekends and holidays. This was a burden for many teachers. As one GLOBE teacher reported, "It has also been difficult at times to collect data on the weekends. Students are not always able to come in since their families have other activities on the weekends (like soccer games that are also occurring at solar noon)." Other teachers reported a more general concern for lack of time, fitting the project into an already packed day. As one GLOBE teacher stated,

> My only problem has been finding enough time! (Isn't that everyone's complaint?) Our schedule is so packed (fifth grade) and there are so many extra programs they are supposed to participate in: DARE, Junior Achievement, Here's Looking at You 2000, H.E.A.T., Ropes, et cetera.

Because of the flexibility of the curriculum, many special-area teachers (such as technology teachers) and resource teachers found telecollaborative projects to be worthwhile, but specialists voiced the problem that they did not see the students regularly enough.

Many of the time and management problems limited the projects' impact, often to just a few students. This was due to schedules that did not coincide with the time for taking readings and the fact that an entire class does not need to go to a weather station to take a single temperature reading. Some teachers used rotating schedules, so different groups of students took readings each day. In one case, more than one group took readings each day, but only one group's readings were official and used for the project. Other teachers simply limited who could participate in the project. A GLOBE participant responded:

> The major concern I have involves the actual number of students who participate in the program. I begin the year training all of my students how to perform the atmospheric protocols. … The protocols must be completed during solar noon. Only three of my five classes take place during the prescribed time. … My other problem is that it doesn't take 30 students to perform the protocols.

Technology

Problems and difficulties with technology were common. However, teachers chose to participate in the projects with a basic understanding of the technological needs of the project, so technology problems were mainly obstacles that teachers found ways to overcome. None of the projects required computer technology more advanced than simple email and web access. Problems included a lack of an Internet connection in the classroom or school and difficulty transmitting information in the appropriate format. In World Weather Watch, information was exchanged with partners via email, but one teacher had difficulty opening her partner's attachments. This teacher could not read the attached file. This problem took several weeks to solve and limited the class's ability to establish a pen-pal relationship. A participant in Signs had difficulty submitting pictures:

> My main problem was my inability to know how to send pictures. The computer technician at my school put them onto a disk for me to transmit from home, but they never got to wherever they were supposed to go.

Although most classrooms today have Internet access, that wasn't true several years ago. A GLOBE teacher reported that he found the students became more involved in the project after the classroom was hooked up to the Internet:

> Last year I was taking the data home and sending it on my home computer. This year we are online at school. … The students have much more ownership this year. Each child gets to enter the data, and then we print out a copy of the completed sheet for them to take home to show their parents. They are amazed that their data is instantaneously sent to Boulder, Colorado.

Although the connection problem might not be as significant today, the issue of ownership by the students is still real and underscores that students will benefit most when they feel like they own the project.

Some teachers find that students could help them with technical problems. For example,

> The first year I taught GLOBE I had two wonderful students who were very strong in science (they also were good on the computer). … I was having trouble at first logging on. They read the instructions and figured out which number was our code and which was our password.

Curriculum

Teachers find more success with projects when the projects match their curricular goals or when their curricula are flexible enough to change or adjust to the objectives of the project. Whenever technology is viewed as an add-on to the curriculum and not integrated with the curriculum, it becomes an extra burden. Several teachers found that the projects helped organize and extend their curricula. One GLOBE teacher responded:

> I don't find that GLOBE detracts from my curriculum since I determine what is in my curriculum. As a matter of fact, it has helped me organize my ecology curriculum around a central theme.

Other teachers found that the projects were worthwhile, but they did not meet their curricular needs. This was most apparent with a teacher who was looking for something very specific that Signs did not provide. His objective was for his "students to discover that kids in the southern hemisphere were reporting increasing temperature/hours of daylight, and corresponding changes in plant activity," while his students were reporting the opposite in the fall. He was disappointed that during the semester he participated in the project, there were no participants from the southern hemisphere. The most successful teachers found that the projects they chose were not add-ons but meshed well with the existing curriculum.

Additionally, matching the grade level you teach to the project can be very important. Different teachers found that the projects were more appropriate with different grade levels. GLOBE offers learning activities for students in a variety of grades, but many teachers found that younger students had trouble understanding the importance of the data, and one teacher reported that some of the older students were bored:

> Younger students (participation ranges from third to tenth grade) had difficulties not only in taking measurements but in understanding the significance of the measurements; some older students became bored with the repetitiveness of taking the same daily measurements.

A few teachers reported problems with students as young as third and fourth grade understanding the significance of the GLOBE data: "This year I have a straight third grade class. In my opinion, they are a little young for most of this program. … For these reasons, I am turning over the program to a fifth grade teacher here at my school. … These third graders are still very focused on themselves." One sixth grade teacher found that his students had similar problems:

> I often wonder if they are able to make connections from their experiences to the use of their submitted data. It tends to get lost once it is typed in. I have not been successful in pulling back their data and comparing it to other GLOBE sites.

When the curriculum and grade-level matches are good, the projects have the best chance of succeeding. A kindergarten teacher found that Signs could help her teach concepts that are difficult for her students: "Everyone is not having the same weather at the same time. Kindergarten children have a hard time with concepts like that."

Communication

Issues of communication were a problem for some teachers. This was true for World Weather Watch, in which classes were partnered with other classes. Partnering provided great benefits to participants with active partners, but those benefits were limited in some cases by partners that did not keep up their communication. A World Weather Watch participant commented that communication, including an electronic discussion board and email with the partner school, were beneficial, although not all schools took full advantage of them:

> It was nice that she included a partner school and a place to share. You always hope that people take advantage of the sharing, but this is a new medium for teachers.

The organizer of the World Weather Watch project expressed her concerns about participant sharing. She was hesitant to match classrooms with partners, but she felt that the benefits outweighed the risks:

> As with any free endeavor, there was a certain amount of attrition. In many instances, I was informed via email that a class would not be able to continue, and I was then able to rematch their partner class. In other instances, the class left high and dry chose not to be rematched but rather to just use the weekly data on the page for their in-class activities. I spent many hours trying to decide if I wanted to match classes for this very reason and decided that with having a partner school came a little more commitment.

Since the project was free and easy to join, not all schools felt the same commitment that they might have if they had paid to join the project or paid for expensive equipment. This created some frustration when partners dropped out of the project.

Other

Many other problems occurred for some of the teachers. Projects have fairly strict time frames and schedules, as do schools. When these schedules are disrupted by problems, telecollaborative projects might not work. The most serious problems were expense and equipment security. Although none of the projects in the study had a registration fee, the GLOBE project required approximately $500 worth of equipment to take proper data readings. Many teachers found support from their schools and school systems. Others sold popcorn.

Security of the equipment became a problem for many teachers. Even locked equipment was occasionally stolen or vandalized, as one GLOBE teacher reported:

> Another problem we encountered was vandalism. Our station is locked, but one of the students didn't lock it securely, and another student took one of the thermometers and hid it. … This year our rain gauge was smashed even though it was within a brick wall.

For every problem with Internet projects, some teachers find that the Internet limits the usefulness of the project, and others find solutions or view problems as opportunities. Almost every teacher reported some kind of problem with every project, but most of them found ways to be successful despite (or sometimes because of) the problems.

Finding Telecollaborative Projects

So far, you have read about different types of projects and seen some examples of projects, but I couldn't possibly list every existing (or future) project in this chapter. Later in the chapter, I'll tell you how to create your own project, but you might want to start by joining an existing project.

This section discusses places to look for existing telecollaborative projects. And when you are ready to create your own project, most of these resources can be used to find telecollaborators.

Global SchoolNet (and project registry)
www.globalschoolnet.org
www.gsn.org/gsh/pr/

> *"Global SchoolNet's mission is to support 21st-century learning and improve academic performance through content-driven collaboration. We engage teachers and K–12 students in meaningful project learning exchanges worldwide to develop science, math, literacy and communication skills, foster teamwork, civic responsibility and collaboration, encourage workforce preparedness and create multi-cultural understanding. We prepare youth for full participation as productive and effective citizens in an increasing global economy."*

The Global SchoolNet project registry (www.gsn.org/gsh/pr/) has been around since 1995 connecting teachers with one another. The registry does not create telecollaborative projects. Instead, it serves as a clearinghouse for project announcements. The registry's search engine allows you to search projects by age, starting date, curriculum area, technology used, or types of collaboration. You can also add keywords to your search to try to search for something specific. Anyone can submit a project to this site, so the number of available projects varies from about 30 to over 100 at any given time.

ePals

www.epals.com

> *"ePals is the leading provider of safe collaborative technology for schools to connect and learn in a protected, project-based learning network. With classrooms in 200 countries and territories, ePals makes it easy to connect learners locally, nationally or internationally."*

ePals allows teachers to create protected and monitored email accounts for their students and connect their students to other registered students. Teachers can control the level of monitoring (including whether to require all incoming and outgoing email to be approved by the teacher before being sent). ePals is more of a platform for collaboration than a project registry. ePals includes a few ready-made projects, which require finding collaborators. Many of these projects involve students from different schools exchanging emails. ePals provides the framework, complete with lesson plans and collaboration tools, but you have to find the collaborators. Fortunately, they make that easy as well. You can find collaborators by visiting the teachers' forum and reading requests for collaborators or writing your own request. Additionally, each classroom in ePals is required to create a classroom profile upon registration. You can search profiles for potential collaborators. (Although the registry has over 100,000 profiles, many were added several years ago and might no longer be active.) However, new profiles are added every day, and the search engine lists the profiles in order of when they were added, starting with the most recent.

ePals is a great place to find collaborators from all over the world. On a recent search, I found 307 profiles from the United States that had been added in the last month as well as (just to give you a random sense of the participants): 17 from Australia, 17 from Canada, 1 from Costa Rica, 3 from Egypt, 21 from France, 1 from Israel, 5 from Russia, 4 from Turkey, and 1 from Zimbabwe. Remember, these numbers are all profiles that are newly added in the last month from a sampling of countries, so you are likely to find many more potential collaborators.

In order to use ePals, you are not required to use one of their ready-made projects. Just like you can search the forums and profiles for collaborators with the ready-made projects, you can also search for collaborators for projects of your own design. Within days of joining ePals, I was contacted by someone who read my profile and was interested in finding ways for our classes to connect.

Kidlink

www.kidlink.org
www.kidlink.org/drupal/about
kidlink.org/drupal/forum

"Kidlink Project is run by a Swedish non commercial organization called Kidlink Association. The project helps children understand their possibilities, set goals for life and develop life-skills. The educational projects are free. The projects do motivate learning, by helping teachers to relate to local curriculum guidelines and to student's personal interests and goals. Kidlink is open for all children and youth in any country up to the age of 15, and for students that are attending secondary school. Most users are between 10–15 years of age. Since the start in 1990, children from 176 countries participated in Kidlink projects."

Kidlink provides a platform for sharing telecollaborative projects. Like ePals, it includes a few ready-made projects, the most popular of which seems to be the Landmark Game. Its most powerful feature for telecollaborative projects is the sharing of project ideas and participation requests through the Kidlink forum.

iEARN

www.iearn.org

"iEARN (International Education and Resource Network) is the world's largest non-profit global network that enables teachers and youth to use the Internet and other technologies to collaborate on projects that enhance learning and make a difference in the world."

Without a membership, you can look around the iEARN website and get information about iEARN projects, but to participate in the projects or forums, you need to become a member. Membership fees vary by country. Currently in the United States, the fee is $100 for an individual teacher and $400 for a school to join for a year. iEARN has several projects (mostly facilitated by teachers) designed to increase global collaboration. Projects can be searched in the Collaboration Centre by title, keyword, subject, age level, and language (many iEARN projects are run in English, but many use other languages).

Many of the projects are publishing projects, such as the Bullying Project (https://media.iearn.org/projects/bullying), where children share their bullying stories for web publication. Other projects involve more direct collaboration, such as the Laws of Life: Virtues Project (https://media.iearn.org/node/109), where children write essays and exchange email about the values they find important.

Flat Classroom Project

www.flatclassroomproject.net
http://flatclassroomproject.ning.com

> *"The concept of a 'flat classroom' is based on the constructivist principle of a multi-modal learning environment that is student-centered and a level playing field for teacher to student and student to teacher interaction.*

> *"The first project was founded in 2006 by two classroom teachers, Julie Lindsay (then in Dhaka, Bangladesh) and Vicki Davis (Camilla, Georgia) and quickly received recognition for the innovative approach of knitting two classrooms together for common, authentic research and production of meaningful, unique multimedia. As of 2012, Lindsay and Davis were still actively involved in the project and working in Beijing (www.flatclassroomproject.net/organizers.html).*

> *"Since the original founding, a grassroots movement of teachers has joined with the original pioneers to continue the original Flat Classroom Project. In addition, other projects have emerged, including Digiteen Project (digital citizenship), Eracism (global debating for cultural understanding) and NetGenEd (emerging technologies)."*

The Flat Classroom Project is less of a project registry and more of a project. However, the project site and the project Ning (http://flatclassroomproject.ning.com) are places to interact with and learn from like-minded teachers who want to use technology to connect classrooms. The project has expanded from the original and now includes more teachers and a few other projects, and they welcome new ideas for projects that align with their goals.

ProjectsByJen

www.projectsbyjen.com

> *"Jennifer Wagner, creator of ProjectsByJen, has been successfully encouraging teachers since 1999 to use online projects in their PK–6*

classrooms. Using various ideas, Jennifer will help you understand how online projects will help you make the most of your time in a variety of ways. Winning numerous awards for her creative ways in encouraging teachers to collaborate, her teaching style is very user friendly, creative, and personable."

This is the site that coordinates projects run by Jennifer Wagner, a teacher who has been running telecollaborative projects since 1999. She has run more than 80 different projects over the years and currently has nine active projects listed on her site, as of this writing (www.projectsbyjen.com/calendar.htm).

Creating Your Own Telecollaborative Projects

Because projects work best when they match your curriculum, you might not find the exact ready-made project you want. In that case, you might decide to create your own. Creating your own project can be challenging and time-consuming, but the rewards can be great because you can design a project that meets your needs exactly. Here are some tips for creating successful projects.

Tip 1 — **Start small.** The perfect project might involve 50 classrooms from 10 different countries. That's a great goal, but it's a bad idea to start out big. If you can benefit from connecting with one or two other classrooms, it is best to start that way and grow the project over time, after you have worked out some of the problems with a small group.

Tip 2 — **Start with someone you know.** Email is great, but nothing beats being able to call up your friend and say, "This isn't working. How can we adjust it?" Just like starting small, it helps to work out the problems with a few people you know before launching a big project. Take the example of the Flat Classroom Project. It started when Vicki Davis, a teacher in Camilla, Georgia, and her friend Julie Lindsay, then a teacher in Bangladesh, got together to have their classes gain a global perspective. The first year, it was just those two teachers. It has now grown into a network of classrooms.

Tip 3 — **Communicate with participants.** A project only works when classrooms get involved and stay involved. Keeping lines of communication open helps teachers remain connected to the project.

Tip 4 — Maintain a timeline. Teachers need to plan, and nothing is worse than not knowing when you need to do what. Some projects require strict timelines, while others can be more flexible. Whatever the requirements of your project are, make them clear to all teachers and students, and stick to whatever timeline you establish.

Tip 5 — Create clear objectives. The easiest way to tell if a project is right for you is to see if its objectives match yours. Teachers will want to know what your project's objectives are before they will sign up and commit.

Tip 6 — Provide closure. After all classrooms have done what they are supposed to do, the project could easily fade away. Be sure to end the project with some sort of closure, such as posting results on the project's website and thanking all the participants.

Nancy Schubert's site, http://nschubert.home.mchsi.com/education/eddevelop.html, hasn't been updated for several years, so links to specific projects are mostly outdated, but she provides a great resource for developing your own telecollaborative project. She offers five key steps to developing a project:

1. Plan

2. Recruit

3. Train

4. Manage

5. Wrap-up

The planning phase is key. You have to be clear about your curricular objectives, your technology requirements, and your timeline. Like any good lesson, you need to know what you want to do before you do it. Unlike a lesson in your classroom, you can't simply change direction in the middle if something isn't working quite right, so planning becomes the most important step.

Once you know what you want to do, it is time to recruit participants. Many of the sites in the previous section are good places to advertise. However, you might have contacts within your school district or outside to help set up the collaboration you want. At a minimum, you will need a clear call-for-participants that lays out the plan. Having a website (or wiki or blog) to provide detailed information and a place for participants to interact is a bonus. It helps to have a registration process so teachers commit themselves to the project and so you can let them know they have been accepted to the project.

Larger projects with minimal interaction can work without formal registration, but registration helps keep the project organized and participants committed. It also helps you to limit participation if too many are interested and to work harder to recruit more if not enough are interested. If you don't know the participants personally, it might help to recruit a few extra because some are likely to drop out.

Once you have participants, be sure to provide whatever training they need. If they need to submit data, a practice run is helpful. If they simply need to exchange emails, it is still helpful to start with introductions to make sure everyone can connect. The training step helps you avoid problems while the project is running and students are depending on their telecollaborators.

Management of the project is very important. Plan a specific timeline, and stick to it. Remind participants of deadlines, thank them for meeting the deadlines, and encourage them to keep up the good work. Making sure everything runs smoothly is a lot of work, but it's the only way to keep your collaborators happy and excited about participating in the project.

Sometimes the difference between a good project and a poor project is how it ends. In the worst case, the project is never completed. Don't let this happen to your project. Work out the problems that will crop up, and make adaptations to bring the project to completion. Once the project does end, thank the participants, distribute the results (via email or your website or both), and keep in touch with everyone. These people are your collaborators and colleagues. They might participate in the project the following year, or they might work with you to create something new and exciting.

Any plan for a telecollaborative project will need the following components, and many will be used for your call-for-participation to advertise your project.

> **Project Title.** The first thing anyone sees is the title of the project, so an interesting and catchy name helps to attract participants.

> **Project Summary.** You will want to create a clear, one- to two-paragraph description of your project that will help potential participants understand what the project is about.

> **Start and End Dates.** Some projects are continuous, but most have a well-defined starting and ending date. Making this clear will help prospective participants decide if they can be part of the project.

> **Number of Classrooms.** You should decide in advance how many participants you need for a successful project and how many total you can handle. Some projects involve two classrooms, while others involve hundreds. A project

comparing the boiling points of water at different elevations won't work very well with just two classrooms, but a project involving deep discussions among students can't handle more than two or three classrooms. Even a project that simply requires classes to send brief snippets of data can easily overwhelm a teacher if there are too many participants.

Age/Grade Range. Be clear about what ages/grades this project is appropriate for.

Curricular Areas. Is this a math project? Is it social studies? List the specific curricular areas for this project. Many projects are interdisciplinary, so you can list more than one area.

Target Audience. Do you need participants from foreign countries, from different geographic locations, with different language skills, and so on? Be clear about what you need.

Project Coordinator. Make sure potential participants know who you are and how to contact you.

Project Website. Having a central place for communication can be very helpful. This can be a traditional website or wiki or blog. It's not required, but this central hub of communication, at a minimum, will organize information and resources about the project and help keep you and your collaborators on track.

Project Objectives. For planning purposes, you will want to have detailed objectives tied to international, national, or local content standards. As you advertise the project, you can list brief summaries of these objectives.

Project Timeline. You will need a detailed timeline, including when classrooms are supposed to do each thing. You certainly can have flexibility built in, but make the expectations clear. You will be counting on participants to meet your timeline, and they will be counting on you and the other participants to cooperate. Plan to email reminders about deadlines.

Communication Plan. Plan for how you will keep in touch with participants, including newly registered participants. Think about what you will post to your website and when, and think about when you will send emails as reminders, thank yous, or general updates. Keeping in touch throughout the project keeps the participants interested.

Closure. Plan for how you will provide closure to the project. Thank the participants. Post results on the website. Get feedback about the success of the project from the participants. Don't let the project simply fade away.

Assessment of Student Objectives. Create a plan for how you will assess your students. Other classrooms do not necessarily need to follow your assessments, but making yours available to them will be helpful.

Evaluation of the Project. How will you know if the project was a success and whether you want to do it again? You will need to decide if the project was successful for your students and for the students in other participating classrooms. Match the results you recorded with your objectives, and survey the participants about their results.

Technology Requirements. Different schools have different technology available to them. Don't assume that every participant will have exactly what you have. Be clear about what is needed to participate in the project in terms of software, hardware, and web tools. Remember that some districts block some Web 2.0 tools that you might want to use in your project.

Activity Structure. Although pinning down one specific activity structure isn't necessary, it is helpful to think about your project in terms of the activity structures described earlier in this chapter. If you know whether the project is a pooled data analysis or a keypal project, listing that can be helpful to prospective participants.

Registration Instructions. Some projects cannot work without registration (e.g., so you can match up classrooms for paired communication), but all projects benefit from it. Although you might not think that you need to have participants register, it is very helpful to know who is participating before you start. You will know whether you have enough interest to run the project at all, and you will know what to expect. Decide what you need to know about the classrooms, and write clear instructions for registering. For example, if you are trying to recruit classrooms from different geographic regions, you will need to know the location (if they are just counting jellybeans, the location might not be important). For a simple project, you might just ask for them to send you an email requesting they be part of the project. For a more complex project, you might create a form on your website or via Google Forms (http://docs.google.com) or Survey-Monkey (www.surveymonkey.com).

Registration Deadline. Set a deadline for registration. People respond to deadlines. Make the deadline clear in your call for participation.

Plans for Expansion. You are likely to start small, but you might have grand ideas. These might change after you run through the project once, but it is helpful to know where you are going with the project. Keep a simple log of notes for your own use throughout and after the project. Ask your collaborators to note their questions, problems, and successes to share with you during and upon completion of the project.

Literature Review. Before completing your plan, you should look for other similar projects. You might decide an existing project meets your needs, but even if you don't, you are sure to learn something from other projects that have used a similar activity structure or have similar objectives.

Call for Participation

After completing the various parts of the plan, you will create a call for participation to advertise your project. This is likely to go on one or more of the sites from the prior section. Each has its own specific format, and many of the parts of the plan listed previously will be listed. Figures 4.1 and 4.2 are two examples of calls for participation.

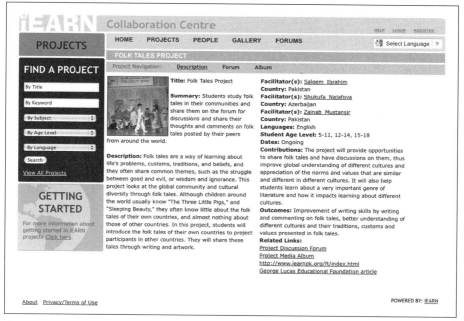

Figure 4.1 An example of a call for participation on the iEARN site.

Basic Project Information

Title: Skype 'R US (ID:3788)

Begin & End Dates: 12/01/10 to 6/01/11

Number of Classrooms: No limit

Age Range: 5 to 12 years

Target Audience: United States

Summary:
> The goal of this project is to collaborate via Skype with a class from each of the 50 states. By video conference via Skype, we hope to enlighten your classroom with information about our community and school as well as develop an understanding of similarities and differences between communities and schools.

Project Details

Project Level: Basic Project

Curriculum Fit: Community Interest; History; Multicultural Studies; Social Studies; Technology

Technologies Used: Audio: files; clips; CDs; tapes; Video: files; clips; CDs; tapes

Collaboration Styles Used: Information Exchange; Intercultural Exchange; Virtual Meeting or Gathering

Full Project Description:
> This project will entail a one time video conference meeting of my class and the participants class. We will utilize Skype to video conference. This video chat can last for as little or as long as desired. During this video chat, we will be asking questions about your community, school and classroom. In addition, we hope to answer any questions for participants. If desired, more than one video chat can occur.

Objectives:
> By collaborating with a classroom we will be able to gain a better understanding about communities, schools and classes from across the United States. We will be able to see what areas are alike and different by completing a video chat.

Project URL: http://https://sites.google.com/site/skyperusiowa/

Registration Information

Registration Status: Open

Registration Dates: 12/01/10 to 6/01/11

Registration Instructions:
> Please contact me to set up a time to collaborate via Skype. I am in the Central time zone. We are hoping to collaborate with a school from each of the 50 states. Please help us achieve our goal and play an integral part along the way.

CLICK HERE to send email to project coordinator.

Project Coordinator Information

Andrew Fenstermaker - (Click to Send EMail)
Penn Elementary
North Liberty, Iowa, United States

Other Projects by Andrew Fenstermaker
> Communities Around the World (Dec 10 - Jun 11)
> Counting Quarters (Feb 10 - May 10) Closed
> Skype 'R US (Dec 10 - Jun 11)

Figure 4.2 A Global SchoolNet call for participation.

Figure 4.1 is from the iEARN Collaboration Centre (http://media.iearn.org/projects) and Figure 4.2 is from the Global SchoolNet Internet Projects Registry (www.globalschoolnet.org/GSH/pr). Visit these sites to view more examples.

Creating your own telecollaborative project is a great way to have a project that meets your exact needs, including your specific objectives and timeline. If you can't find a project that is just what you want, consider starting your own.

Conclusion

Telecollaborative projects help expand your classroom, bringing in different perspectives and different data. It's normal for many students to be stuck in the here and now and to have trouble thinking about the bigger picture—the larger world outside their own homes, schools, and communities. Making real connections outside of the classroom can help students expand their horizons and their understanding and become true 21st-century learners. Think about what your classroom lacks and what it can gain from a connection to others, and then use the Internet to find what you're lacking. Telecollaborative projects provide data and diversity that you and your students do not have the resources to provide on your own. Reach out and break down the walls of the classroom to see beyond your students' narrow focus.

Exercises

1. Think about your curriculum, and think of two or three areas that might benefit from a connection with other classes via the Internet. Brainstorm ideas for projects in that curricular area. What activity structures might you use for the projects?

2. Explore some of the projects listed in this chapter and some of the sources of projects. Find four projects that might benefit your classroom.

3. Prepare an outline for a telecollaborative project, including filling in the list of items that you need to design your own project.

References

Friedman, T. (2007). *The world is flat: A brief history of the twenty-first century* (3rd ed.). New York, NY: Picador.

Harris, J. (1998*a*). Virtual architecture: Designing and directing curriculum-based telecomputing. Eugene, OR: International Society for Technology in Education.

Harris, J. (September 1998*b*). Curriculum-based telecollaboration: Using activity structures to design student projects. *Learning & Leading with Technology, 26*(1), 6–15.

Harris, J. (2010). Telelearning activity types. Retrieved December 13, 2010, from Texas Technology Integration Professional Development Corps website: http://txtipd.wm.edu/documents/TelelearningActivityTypes.pdf

Marcovitz, D. M. (1999). What really happens in classroom Internet projects. In J. Willis, J. D. Price, S. McNeil, B. Robin, & D. Willis (Eds.), *Technology and Teacher Education Annual* (pp. 1751–1763). Charlottesville, VA: Association for the Advancement of Computing in Education.

Peters, L. (2009). *Global education: Using technology to bring the world to your students.* Eugene, OR: International Society for Technology in Education.

Richardson, W. (2010, May 31). Nervous writing/well-trained teachers [Blog post]. Retrieved from http://weblogg-ed.com/2010/nervous-writing-well-trained-teachers

Stoll, C. (1999). *High-tech heretic: Why computers don't belong in the classroom and other reflections by a computer contrarian*. New York, NY: Doubleday.

CHAPTER FIVE

Web 2.0

Back when I was a kid (actually, back when I was in graduate school) in the early 1990s, we had the web. We didn't call it Web 1.0, but we could have called it Internet 2.0 because it was really an evolutionary leap from earlier applications on the Internet, such as email, Gopher, FTP (File Transfer Protocol), IRC (Internet Relay Chat), and newsgroups. In Web 1.0, most people were consumers who would read information provided by others. To be a producer, you needed some technical skill with HTML, and you needed server space for your web pages. Lots of people, including many teachers, created web pages, but few individuals stuck with keeping them updated. Large and medium businesses all had websites, and thousands of individuals had websites that they maintained. But website maintenance was hard, so a relatively small percentage did more than dabble.

Throughout the 1990s, many tools were created that made it easier to put things on the web. Some websites had limited commenting or feedback capability. Word-processor-like tools, such as Microsoft FrontPage, allowed users to create web pages more easily. By 2000, most schools had a website, sometimes professionally maintained, but usually maintained by a teacher. However, relatively few individuals had a significant web presence at this point.

In the late 1990s and early 2000s, some new tools began to emerge on the web. Among the first easy-to-use web-based tools were Open Diary, LiveJournal, and blogger.com. (Blogger, by the way, is now owned by Google and is one of the most popular blogging sites.) Like many good tools, these tools didn't do much that couldn't be done before, but they made it much easier. Suddenly, in a few minutes, individuals with no technical skills could create websites. And because it was so easy, people actually did, and they kept doing it.

And Web 2.0 was born. Although there is no strict definition of Web 2.0, some people refer to it as the Read-Write Web. No longer is it a small elite that can and/or will create information on the web. It is now open to everyone. Web 2.0 is about interaction and participation, not merely consumption.

Most Web 2.0 tools are online. You go to a website, such as bubbl.us (http://bubbl.us), and start creating and sharing material. However, Web 2.0 is really about anything that makes it easy to create and interact on the web. In fact, my definition of Web 2.0 is any tool that is easy enough that you will actually use it on a regular basis to create and interact. If it's a little too hard or inconvenient for you to use it regularly, it's not Web 2.0. That means that tools like Jing (www.techsmith.com/jing.html) aren't necessarily online tools, but they are really easy to install and use to help you create projects and interact online.

Most Web 2.0 tools are free. Many, such as Jing and bubbl.us, have free versions that are quite good and premium versions that cost money. If you are a regular user of a tool, you might want to splurge for the version that requires payment, but you probably don't need it. The goal is to find tools that you can actually continue to use and that will help your students learn.

Now if Web 2.0 tools are free and easy enough for you to use, they are certainly easy enough for your students to use (most of them already do). The real power is that you can worry less about the technical requirements and think more about how these tools can help your students learn. Rather than thinking, "How can I navigate the expensive and difficult tools to make videos for (or with) my students?" you can be thinking, "What will making a video do for my students?" Just remember that Web 2.0 tools are often about quick and easy rather than perfect. It is still a lot of work to make a perfect video, and even though the technical aspects are fairly easy (pop out your FlipCam or iPod Touch, hit record, plug it into your computer, and upload it to YouTube), thinking about the writing, the speaking/acting, and making it work with your curriculum are still challenging.

This chapter will describe a few Web 2.0 tools. Many others are mentioned in passing throughout the chapter and the book. If you see a tool mentioned, feel free to jump to the web and try it out. You'll probably have done something fun in 15 minutes and have thought of a dozen classroom ideas in 30 minutes.

One word of caution: many schools block a lot of Web 2.0 applications. Be sure to try the tools in your school before you spend too much time planning to use them in your classroom. If a tool is blocked, an alternative, comparable tool might work. Additionally, you might be able to petition your school or school system to have a particular tool unblocked. Arm yourself with an educational plan for how you want to use the tool, and get to know your school's or school system's process for getting it approved. Some bureaucratic systems have complex processes that take many months, while some schools have a tech person down the hall who can take care of it on the spot.

Beyond Motivation

One of the key reasons many people suggest that teachers should use Web 2.0 tools with students is motivation. In "A New Way to Publish—The Rise of Web 2.0," a teachertube.com PowerPoint presentation with audio, creator Suzie Vesper says, "Web 2.0 technology motivates children through access to a wider audience" (Suziea, 2007, slide 3). Although this is true, it is only part of the story.

Once you get past the new and exciting nature of Web 2.0 (the motivating part), some of the tools have real substance. The most powerful thing about Web 2.0 tools is that they are easy to use. Their ease of use helps to bend the curve of cost to reward. Imagine that you are a budding writer and the tool you have is a hammer and chisel. Your writing career is likely to be over before it starts because too much time and energy are spent struggling to write anything. Now, imagine your medium is paper and pen or a typewriter or a computer. You might not be a better writer, but the costs are minimal to try. Next, imagine that you want to share your writing with others. Paper and pen are a good start. The copy machine will help. But a blog will make the cost of sharing very small: zero in monetary costs (if you own or have access to a computer that connects to the Internet) and next to nothing in time and energy beyond actually writing what you want.

However, a motivating, cost-effective technology is not enough. The next powerful aspect of Web 2.0 technology is that it is often collaborative. A wiki can be viewed as an easy way to make a web page to share with others (it is), but with little time and energy, it can be a way to build a collaborative document. If multiple people are working on something together, this powerful Web 2.0 tool can facilitate that. This isn't to say that all writing has to be collaborative, but Web 2.0 tools have made it easy to do collaborative writing (within a classroom or around the world). Just as a teacher with only hammers and chisels isn't going to think about asking students to write essays, a teacher without collaboration tools isn't going to explore collaborative writing. But when writing with others becomes easy to do, teachers can find ways to help their students that are appropriate. That's not just because it's motivating but because it's authentic and useful and, when done well, can help students learn.

In summary, when the tools to do something are difficult to use, you are unlikely to use them even if using them would have great benefits. As the tools become easier to use, new pedagogical opportunities open up. Web 2.0 provides a range of easy-to-use tools and, thus, opens a whole new pedagogical landscape.

Changing Everything and Nothing

We are always looking for the tool or technique that will change everything in education. I'll let you in on a little secret: there is no Web 2.0 tool that is going to change everything. I have heard educators praise blogs, wikis, Prezi, Museum Box, Diigo, Ning, and VoiceThread as "the tool that's going to transform learning." The secret is that there is no single tool that will transform education. There is nothing wrong with any of these tools. They are all great, but none of them "changes everything." Their power is that they will all help you accomplish tasks that you might want to do.

You can't organize a meaningful curriculum, for example, around blogging. On the other hand, you might want to organize your curriculum around writing. In that case, a blog might help you by making it easy for your students to share their writing, within the class or outside the class, and receive feedback from the community of learners and readers. Does the blog change everything? No, but the blog helps you do what you want to do.

If you want to turn your writing and feedback into multimedia, VoiceThread might work for you by allowing comments in text, picture, audio, and video format. To view a great example of the use of VoiceThread in a collaborative project, go to http://sswiech.blogspot.com/2012/02/collaborative-voicethread-project.html.

Does VoiceThread change everything? No, but it adds to what you are already doing, and it is cheap. It is also very easy to incorporate into your classroom. Don't plan to build your whole curriculum around VoiceThread. Plan to build a lesson or unit around VoiceThread if you can see that it will help you do what you want to do. Additional suggestions are discussed later in this chapter under Podcasts.

> ## GETTING STARTED WITH VOICETHREAD
>
> I encourage you to turn to the chapter that gives detailed instructions about how to use VoiceThread and incorporate it into your classroom. Wait! There isn't such a chapter in this book; it's too easy.
>
> For complete instructions, go to voicethread.com and register as a member. If you want to learn about how it works first, go to the site, hit the Browse button, and select the short video titled "What's a VoiceThread?"

Constructivist, Collaborative, and Student Centered?

Since the advent of educational technology, every new tool has been touted as the new thing that is going to save education (see, for example, Cuban, 1986). Additionally, someone claims that every new technology is constructivist, collaborative, and/or student centered. I have no problem with a good lecture. Just don't try to tell me that because that lecture was converted to PowerPoint (or Prezi), it is now somehow a constructivist lesson.

We want to use Web 2.0 tools because they are easy and they help us do something we want to do. Sometimes they facilitate collaboration or constructivism, and sometimes they don't. For example, tools like Scriblink (http://scriblink.com) and Dabbleboard (http://dabbleboard.com) are collaborative online white boards. Inside the classroom, they are neat tools, but as you expand your classroom beyond your physical location, they can become powerful collaboration tools. Multiple people in different locations can work together on a common whiteboard with drawing, picture, and equation tools. If they facilitate collaboration, they are collaborative. If they are used to help a teacher give a lecture, they are not.

A Sampling of Web 2.0 Tools

The rest of this chapter will review a few Web 2.0 tools. There are thousands of individual tools and several broad categories of tools. You can find a listing of many different tools at GoToWeb20 (www.go2web20.net), and you can find brief descriptions of many tools for schools at Web 2.0: Cool Tools for Schools (http://cooltoolsforschools.wikispaces.com).

Some of the main categories of Web 2.0 tools are blogs, microblogs, wikis, podcasts, social bookmarks, and social networking. Many tools can be classified in one of these categories, but Web 2.0 is far too new and fluid to have fixed categories, so don't worry if you find a tool and can't classify it in one of those ways. New tools are being created all the time, and many defy categorization.

Blogs

One of the most common Web 2.0 tools is the blog (web log). At its core, it is simply a digital journal. But like all good innovations, its power comes from the way it differs from a basic journal that leads to new directions. If it is just a digital journal, its value in the classroom is limited to whether it is easier for students to write on a blog or write on paper. Will Richardson (2010) gives a thorough description of what blogs are and how they can be used in the classroom. He suggests that blogging is powerful because it extends the relevance of writing beyond the classroom, allows collaboration with others outside the classroom, creates an archive of all student writing, democratizes the conversation by giving everyone an equal voice, allows for the development of expertise on a single subject, and helps students analyze and manage knowledge in an "ever-expanding information society" (pp. 26–28). Does blogging really do all this? Well, blogging can do all this, and blogging facilitates doing all this, but blogging doesn't magically make every one of these things happen.

This is a key lesson in innovation in the classroom. If you are reading this book and looking for a tool that will come to your classroom and change everything, you need to stop and rethink what innovation is all about. Innovation comes into an existing social context (your school and/or classroom, for example) and interacts with the people in that context and the culture of that context (Marcovitz, 2006). If you want your students to journal, the blogs they write will be journals. However, if you want your students to think deeply and make connections, you (the really great teacher) might be able to leverage blogging into a tool that can help you do that. Perhaps the technology is more than just a simple tool, but you and your students (and possibly their audience on the web) are the chief actors that make the tool powerful.

Richardson (2010) presents a more powerful vision of blogging as a way for students to leverage the power of blogging to promote critical thinking. The audience, the interaction, and the ability to link to sources are features of the blog that allow you to help your students go beyond journaling to using their writing and interaction to make complex connections with linked material. In Chapter Two, Critical Information Literacy, I described mapping a domain of knowledge. A blog could simply be a series of entries to link to a variety of sources about a particular subject, or it could be a growing analysis of the interconnections of various sources with feedback from readers, whose comments help to enhance the analysis. It's not the only tool that could help with this analysis and synthesis of complex material, but it is one tool that makes it easier.

This doesn't mean that your first venture into blogging has to be the most powerful thing you have ever done in the classroom. There is nothing wrong with a little online journaling, even if it doesn't provide for deep thinking. As you and your students get more comfortable with blogging, you can expand what you do by taking advantage of different parts of what is potentially powerful about blogs. For example, my students were blogging about a book we were reading, and the book raised the subject of the role of libraries in the 21st century, particularly with underserved populations. I was able to bring an inner-city librarian into the conversation to comment on the discussion and share his insights into how inner-city libraries serve their clients. This is just one example of how blogging and communicating via the Internet can help leverage your and your students' connections beyond the classroom walls.

Elementary Blogging

Jacklyn Mueller

Last year I created a class blog through Edublogs (http://edublogs.org) for my students to use in our school computer lab. Creating one blog for my class seemed easier for them to use since they are younger. My students had just finished creating a book review podcast in their technology class. So I decided to have each student write a review of a different book from our class library on our class blog. I wanted the students to share their favorite books they've read in hopes of encouraging other students in the class to read it.

The students really enjoyed participating and reading each other's responses. It was a great way for them to learn about new books in our classroom library. With second graders it does take some time to introduce and explain the process of adding a comment. I was able to use the LCD projector to walk the students through it step by step. Second graders also need time and some help with typing. I personally think it may be difficult to have kindergarteners or first graders blogging without additional teacher support.

Jacklyn Mueller is a second grade teacher at Longfellow Elementary School in Howard County, Maryland. She used blogging with her students to create brief book reviews. To simplify the process for second graders, she created the blog entry, and the students used the comments for their writing. (See Box 5.1. See also Mueller's second grade class blog at http://jacklyn7.edublogs.org.)

Chapter Four, Telecollaborative Projects, describes projects that make connections with other classrooms. A blog is one tool that can accomplish this. Students can work jointly on blogs with students in other classrooms or comment on each other's blogs.

Richardson (2010) argues that the real power of blogs comes with making connections and analyzing. Scott Rosenberg (2010) makes a convincing argument that links are an important part of reading and writing. He argues that badly constructed links are distracting and problematic, but well-constructed links make a text much more powerful.

This leads to two issues: reading and writing. We must learn to read links better (see, for example, Burbules & Callister, 2000) so we can tell when links are useful and how to use them, and we need to learn to write links better so our links are useful. Blogging is one tool that can help our students read and write links as a part of a serious analysis of a subject.

Many options for blogging in the classroom exist. The simplest blogging tool is Blogger (www.blogger.com). All you have to do is go there and sign up for a blog. Using this tool requires an email address, so it might not be the right choice for student blogging. Many schools and school systems already have course delivery systems like Blackboard and Moodle that have blogging tools built into them. With these systems, the students are already in the system, so email addresses don't need to be used to add accounts, and instructors can keep the blogs private for registered students only or make them public. Because they default to being private, teachers should be sure to make them public if they want to take advantage of the power of connections beyond the classroom. Some schools and districts subscribe to blogging tools like Edublogs (http://edublogs.org). With a subscription, students can be automatically registered via the school. Without a subscription, individual teachers and students can sign up for a free Edublogs account without using an email address. However, without an email address, password resets aren't allowed (and you can count on students to forget their passwords). Another easy choice is Kidblog (http://kidblog.org). This simple blogging tool allows teachers to set up blogging for students in a class without requiring student email.

Remember that one advantage of blogging is making connections beyond the classroom walls, so you will want to set the settings so others can read your students' posts. Be sure to check with your school's policies about safety requirements, including what information can be posted online (such as first names, last names, pictures, etc.). Also, be sure that you remind your students of safety rules, like not giving out personal information, such as addresses or phone numbers, as well as other acceptable uses (possibly outlined in your school's acceptable use policy—AUP). Set the settings on the blogs to suit your needs, particularly who is allowed to comment and whether comments must be approved before posting. It is rare that outsiders post inappropriate comments on student blogs, but it can happen, and you should decide in advance whether you want to monitor the comments to delete inappropriate ones after they are posted or if you want to moderate all comments, which requires you to approve all of them before they appear online.

Finally, if students are blogging, it will be most powerful if the teacher is also participating, by commenting on students' blogs, making connections from one blog to another, and recognizing good blogging for the whole class. Sometimes, the students will take off with blogging with little encouragement from the teacher, but most of the time it will take active teacher involvement and positive reinforcement to ensure that the tool remains exciting and continues to meet the curricular needs of the class.

Microblogs (Twitter)

A microblog is similar to a regular blog, but each posting is limited to 140 characters. This isn't the place to make deep connections about content. However, it can be a good way to connect people, and, in an educational context, it can be a way to establish a personal learning network. The primary microblogging tool is Twitter (http://twitter. com). Twitter blog entries are referred to as tweets. Many people simply tweet random thoughts or status updates ("I'm doing laundry"). However, it can be a quick way to create a network. You can simply follow people who share your interests. You might, for example, follow Will Richardson (http://twitter.com/willrich45), Dean Shareski (http://twitter.com/shareski), Gary Stager (http://twitter.com/garystager), Vicki Davis (http://twitter.com/coolcatteacher), Lawrence Lessig (http://twitter.com/lessig), or the United States Department of Education (http://twitter.com/usedgov). Because the messages are short (unless, of course, they are links to longer messages or blog entries), it is easy to keep up with the reading. Or you can tweet regularly and try to build your own following. Many people use Twitter for crowdsourcing by posting a question and letting their followers help them answer it. The power of microblogging is not yet clear for traditional classrooms, but it is a great tool for lifelong learning. If you want to look for other educators on Twitter, check out Twitter 4 Teachers (http://twitter4teachers. pbworks.com) and add your name to the list under a subject that interests you.

Wikis

A wiki is simply a website with multiple authors. Because wikis tend to come with easy tools to build the website (no HTML required although many allow editing in HTML for the techies), many teachers have used wikis in place of web pages. In no time, you can go to Wikispaces (www.wikispaces.com) and create a wiki. If all you want is a web page, it's not a bad way to go, but that leaves out the collaborative aspect of wikis.

The power of wikis is in the collaboration. Multiple people can contribute to a project. With this in mind, you could set up a wiki for your whole class or set up group wikis so that small groups of students can work together editing the same document. Because wikis are in cyberspace, the group editing can extend beyond the classroom and be a tool for managing a telecollaborative project.

Wikipedia (www.wikipedia.org) is the ultimate example of a collaborative effort. It is an online encyclopedia in which everything is written by the users. You might not want to open up your class wiki to the entire world to edit, but you can set it up with access for whomever you want.

One of the great features of all wiki tools is the history feature. It allows you to look back at previous versions of the wiki to see what has changed. This is an invaluable tool for a teacher. If something gets totally messed up, you can revert the wiki back to an earlier version. Additionally, you can look back and see the contributions of each member of a group, as the history saves who did what to the wiki.

As an example, Chuck Moore, a language arts teacher, has his students use the online tools to make connections to other material related to the book the class is reading. (Moore's wiki can be viewed at http://pooteeweet.pbworks.com/w/page/16480414/ FrontPage.)

> One of Moore's classes recently read Kurt Vonnegut's *Slaughterhouse-Five*, and he cited examples of how students were to access the traditional course reading guide but in addition, they also were able to create links to Vonnegut's website, including the novel's reviews and information about the bombing of Dresden, Germany—a key element of the book's plot. This online component allowed students to quickly grasp the book's historical elements, which, in turn, helped them develop a deeper understanding of the book's content, he said. (Fanuko, 2010)

Like a blog, the power doesn't come from simply writing something and putting it on the web; it comes from the ease of making connections. And, specifically for a wiki, the power comes from the ease of doing that with a group of people.

Meredith Jones, a third grade teacher in Baltimore County, Maryland, has been experimenting with Web 2.0, including wikis and VoiceThread. Read about her experience with her "Literature Circle Wiki" in Box 5.2.

In addition to the wiki tools that are now built into course-delivery systems (like Moodle and Blackboard), some popular wiki tools can be found at Wikispaces (www.wikispaces.com), PBworks (http://pbworks.com), and Wetpaint (www.wetpaintcentral.com). Each of these offers a free account with limitations and a pay account that has more features, including options for schools or school systems to purchase large multiuser licenses. Although it is technically not a wiki, Google Docs (http://docs.google.com) has many of the same features of wiki. At its core, it is a place to create collaboratively-edited documents. Google Docs takes it a step further by allowing editing of word processor documents, spreadsheets, and presentations (mostly compatible with Microsoft Office documents). It is also regularly adding features within each document type as well as other document types (it now has drawing capabilities and forms).

Box 5.2

Literature Circle Wiki

Meredith Jones

I've also been experimenting a lot with wikis this year with my class. I began a wiki more as a way to communicate and discuss books with my reading class. Since then, I've given my students more access to editing the site and having more control over it.

On the main site, I have links to different areas of the wiki. At the top, there are links to different literature circle books where students can post and respond to one another. At the bottom, there are general links to a website where students can recommend books that they are reading at home to their classmates, a class play that we have been writing, and some poll creation pages.

What I mostly like about the wiki is that students can collaborate with one another and have control of their own learning. They can also be used to collaborate with other classes telecollaboratively. For instance, they can be used to communicate and learn together.

Instead of a teacher-centered class, I am able to have a more student-centered discussion, where I can make comments or question students as I find necessary. In this way, students are responsible for questioning one another and gathering information to help enhance discussion.

Rachel Cohen, a technology integration teacher at New Town Elementary School in Owings Mills, Maryland, has her fifth grade students use Google Docs for easy peer editing. See Box 5.3, In the Cloud. See also an example of peer-reviewed work at http://tinyurl.com/RachelGoogle.

Box 5.3

In the Cloud

Rachel Cohen

We used the Google account I created for my school, and students were able to upload the pieces they had written in their classroom. Once students had uploaded their writing pieces, we were able to create a link where students could access the work and peer review their classmates' work without logging into a Google account of their own. Students were assigned to peer review two different writing pieces for students in their class. I showed students how they could use the comment feature to identify any changes they thought should be made to the document. By using this feature they would not have to alter the student's current work. They were also able to use this feature to give praise or suggestions to the student.

Podcasts

The word podcast combines the words *iPod* and *broadcast*, but really it is just an audio or video (sometimes called vodcast) recording on the computer that can be listened to or watched on an iPod, cell phone, or computer. It can be shared on a website, blog, wiki, or email message, or it can be placed on a site dedicated to that purpose, such as VoiceThread or YouTube. Podcasts can be created with special tools, such as Audacity (both Mac and Windows), GarageBand (Mac), or Jing (Mac and Windows), while some of the special-purpose sites, such as VoiceThread, Animoto and PodOmatic, allow you to record right on the site. In addition, many devices can be used to create podcasts besides the computer, including cell phones, inexpensive video cameras (see, for example, www.theflip.com), and iPods (some have the capability built in, and others require an attachment). Because these tools are cheap and easy, they have made it possible for all of us to make podcasts whenever we like. You can see this by the proliferation of silly videos on sites like YouTube. Some of these are sophisticated serial productions, but many are spur-of-the-moment one-off creations.

Before we discuss how you can use these tools in your classroom, you should pick a tool and play with it to see just how easy it is to create something. For audio, you will need a microphone on your computer. Many computers now have microphones built into them. If yours doesn't, you can get an external microphone for very little money. However, some sites, like Voki (http://voki.com), Blabberize (http://blabberize.com), and Voice-Thread (http://voicethread.com), allow you to record by phone, and some, like Voki and Blabberize, will speak what you type so you can even try this without a microphone. Just go to one of these sites and try it out. If you type what you want read, it should take you less than two minutes to create something simple.

As a teacher, your goal isn't to create a series of silly videos; you want to create something useful. Two ways to use this technology are from a teacher-centered perspective and from a student-centered perspective. As a teacher, there are many things that you might find easier to explain by speaking instead of writing. You might even find more things that are easier to show. These things can be done to answer student questions, explain something, or simply have material covered in class available for review. Some teachers bring video cameras (or just a cell phone with this capability) with them wherever they go and make recordings to use with their classes. For example, imagine you are visiting a grocery store and want to get the best price. If it were really easy, you might make a quick video right there with the products and prices in front of you to explain how you can compare prices by dividing the price by the package size to get the cost per ounce (or cookie or liter). If you want a professional Hollywood video, you'll need to spend hours shooting various takes and editing. But getting your point across to your students will only take five minutes. See, for example, www.youtube.com/watch?v=ExLii5t1QL8.

If what you want to show is on your computer, screencasting tools, such as Jing (www.techsmith.com/jing), allow you to record whatever is happening on your screen. I have done this to answer a question where typing a description would take longer and be less effective than just showing what I want to show. Additionally, screencasting can be used in place of class lectures by simply posting the lecture to the web for students to watch on their own time. Jonathan Bergmann and Aaron Sams, two science teachers in Colorado, have some excellent examples of this at their site (http://mast.unco.edu/vodcasting). They use a concept they call the "flipped classroom" to turn the classroom around (Bergmann & Sams, 2012). Students acquire the knowledge they need via podcasts, vodcasts, and online texts while they're outside of class (homework). When they're in class, they work through issues and problems (material that would have been assigned as homework in traditional classrooms) with the teacher assisting as needed and giving students a lot of individual attention. Teacher-centered podcasting can be a valuable tool because there are times when the teacher needs to get information across.

If this can be done in a more fun, efficient, and effective way, it not only makes the teacher-centered classroom better, it also creates more student-centered opportunities.

Podcasting as a student-centered tool is a way for your students to create their own podcasts. Podcasters can use this tool to demonstrate their competency with the subject matter, to help other students understand what the podcast creators already understand, and to motivate themselves by presenting the material to a wider audience. The tools are easy, however, the process can be very time consuming. Teachers can often create quick, spur-of-the-moment podcasts to explain things, but as a student assignment, podcasts will require group work to research content, write scripts, and produce the podcast. As with any technology, students can get carried away with the noncurricular aspects, such as background music, and provide a shallow treatment of the content, so your job is to keep them on track.

Although there are a lot of fun uses of podcasts, some of the most powerful come in the context of foreign language and English language learner (ELL) classrooms, subjects that lend themselves most powerfully to actual speaking and listening. Although many university instructors have institutional support to take advantage of podcasting (see, for example, "Podcasting Enables 24/7 Foreign Language Study," Cain, 2007), the technology is now easy enough for K–12 teachers to create their own podcasts. As a teacher, you might be interested in having your students converse with native speakers of a foreign language. This can be done with interactive video through tools such as Skype (http://skype.com), but you might find the safety and logistical concerns to be too much. Using podcasting by having your students listen to foreign language podcasts and record their own can be a good substitute for real interactive video.

VoiceThread can be a powerful tool for brief discussions, especially as reactions to concepts. Two excellent times for using this are for before and after class discussions. You might post a paper or a brief reading to help focus your students and get their initial reactions. VoiceThread can help frame what you do in class by giving you a sense of where your students are starting, triggering their background knowledge. As a summative tool, you could ask specific questions to find out if your students understand what you intended from class (or a reading or a unit or anything else). It might also be used for grading purposes or to give you feedback on whether you accomplished what you wanted and are ready to go on. You could have students be in charge of summarizing and asking questions for each class. You will know if the summarizing students understood the concept by the kinds of questions they ask, and you will know if the rest of the class got it by their answers.

For safety reasons, you might not want to have your students use their pictures or videos of themselves in podcasts or vodcasts. You might choose to use podcasts (voice only) or animation sites like Voki (http://voki.com). Some sites, like VoiceThread, suggest that users post pictures of themselves. As an alternative, avatars can be drawn in paint programs, or screenshots can be used from animation programs like Voki. Although there are free avatar-creating sites, such as DoppelMe (www.doppelme.com), you have to watch for pictures you might find inappropriate at many of them.

Janet Johnston, a science teacher at Harper's Choice Middle School in Howard County, Maryland, has had her students use GarageBand to create podcasts: "Each student pair was given one cell organelle and a sample script. The students had to tell what the cell part's function was in the life of the cell, and then relate it to an everyday object. The students also needed to give a reason why that cell organelle related to the object." Johnston edited all the podcasts together to make a complete podcast for each class. As this was her first attempt at podcasting, she said she ran into many technical problems and found that the project took longer than anticipated for the students to complete, but podcasting helped them think more deeply about their cell organelle and provided a great study guide about the complete cell for all her students.

Julia Zimmerman, a fourth grade teacher at St. Ursula School in Parkville, Maryland, has used podcasts to have her students do a mock interview with fictional characters from the books they read. An example interview with Robin Hood can be found at http://jjk42.podomatic.com/player/web/2010-06-14T15_11_27-07_00. Zimmerman recommends the free booklet, *Podcasting for Teachers and Students* (2009), by Tony Vincent (http://learninginhand.com/storage/podcasting_images/Podcasting_Booklet. pdf) for step-by-step instructions about how to create a podcast, and she uses PodOmatic (www.podomatic.com) to upload and share her podcasts. This kind of interview requires just as much work from students, including more authentic writing, and can require more higher-level thinking skills than for a traditional book report. Zimmerman found that her students enjoyed creating podcasts more than writing regular book reports because of the technology, the collaborative work, and the authentic writing.

Podcasts and vodcasts are great classroom tools that provide another medium for students to share their writing. Traditional written work is often the best assignment for particular tasks, but sometimes students will learn more from creating and performing a script with their own voices, computer voices, videos, and/or animations.

Social Bookmarking

Will Richardson (2010) describes Web 2.0 as a way to develop your personal learning network. One of the earliest Web 2.0 ways to do this is via social bookmarking.

Everyone is familiar with a bookmark or a favorite in your browser (going to the Bookmarks or Favorites menu in your browser and choosing to add a bookmark or favorite). This is great for keeping track of what you find interesting on the web and want to be able to return to easily. However, when you do this, it stops with you. No one else can see your bookmarks. In the early days of the web, I exported my bookmarks as a web page and edited them in HTML to make a website to share with my students. This was an early form of social bookmarking, but it was difficult to do in the first place and difficult to maintain (editing the website every time I wanted to add or delete a bookmark). With particular tools, such as iGoogle (www.google.com/ig), Delicious (www.delicious.com), and iKeepBookmarks (http://ikeepbookmarks.com), you can save your bookmarks online and easily share them with others. Additionally, toolbars can make it as easy to add new bookmarks to your site as it is to add them to your browser. You can set up pages on specific topics and annotate them for your students. As you develop a personal learning network, you might regularly connect to others' social bookmarking sites about topics that interest you.

Diigo (www.diigo.com) takes the idea of social bookmarking a step further. Not only does it allow you to create your own public set of bookmarks, it also allows you to highlight and annotate the pages and create discussions about the pages. In your classroom, you could find a useful page for your students, highlight the important parts, and add notes of your own. You could turn this into a collaborative activity by having groups of your students do the highlighting and annotating to analyze and synthesize the knowledge on that and other pages.

As the web constantly evolves, purpose-built social-bookmarking tools are developing. One example is Goodreads (www.goodreads.com). This is a social bookmarking tool for people to share their opinions of the books they have read. In 2012, Pinterest (www.pinterest.com), an online pinboard, has become the hot new social bookmarking site.

Social bookmarking is another example of something that is not earth shattering yet powerful because it is easy to use. If you aren't inclined to share favorite sites with students or colleagues, social bookmarking won't make you want to do it. But if you like to share interesting information online, you can do it so easily with these tools that you are likely to use them often.

Social Networking

If you haven't heard of social networking (Facebook, MySpace, Bebo, Google+, and others), then you must have been living on a technological desert island for the past several years. Social networks are places for people to connect with other people. Each person creates a profile and connects with friends and their profiles. Depending on settings, friends might be able to see more detailed information about their friends. Additionally, friends can be notified when their friends on the network do certain things. These actions might take place within the system, such as writing a new status message or updating their relationship status. Additionally, some social networks let you connect to activities outside the system by tagging articles, web pages, blog entries, or even online purchases so your friends can see what you like. Social networks allow private and public messages between friends. Many also have applications, such as polls and games. New things are being added all the time.

Most of what is done with social networks, such as on Facebook (www.facebook.com), is social. Sites like LinkedIn (www.linkedin.com) are more for developing business contacts than social contacts, but educational uses are harder to come by. As time goes on, more educational uses of social networks are likely to come about, but for now, I'll describe three educational issues: safety, impersonations, and closed networks.

Safety is largely discussed elsewhere in this book, but it is worth repeating. Children who use social networks should understand that what they post is likely to be public or made public, it is likely to last online for a very long time, and it is possible that it will be used against them in the future. Teenagers have a false sense of invincibility and are likely to do things that they regret later in life; in fact, that is part of growing up. However, with a permanent record of their actions, they need to be cautious about what they share online.

An interesting example of the possibilities of impersonations on Facebook is a Facebook page about World War II events and relationships originally posted as a joke, www.collegehumor.com/article:1802364. (You need to be a member of Facebook to view this.) Students can study countries, fictional characters, or real characters, and create Facebook pages about them instead of writing reports. They can then interact with each other in the role of that character. Imagine your students writing Facebook pages for 19th-century artists as they discuss each other's artwork. Many social networks are likely to be blocked by school firewalls, but remember that students are drawn to interactive technologies like these and allowing them to interact in this way could bring out many reluctant learners and help students make new and interesting connections to the material.

One way that social networks are being used widely in education is with private social networks like Ning (www.ning.com) and Edmodo (www.edmodo.com). Edmodo is free. Ning used to be a free service, but, as of June 2010, it started charging a membership fee. However, educators can still sign up for a free Ning Mini for Educators network by visiting http://about.ning.com/pearsonsponsorship. Ning is a way to create your own private social network. If you already have a personal Facebook account, you probably don't want to "friend" all your students and colleagues. In fact, your school might have a policy forbidding you from friending any of your students. The alternative is to set up a Ning for your classroom or your learning community. This allows the rich interaction that a social network allows while keeping the network focused on a particular purpose. As an additional part of your personal learning network, you might join the ISTE Community Ning (www.iste-community.org). As part of a particular project, you might join the Flat Classroom Project Ning (http://flatclassroomproject.ning.com).

Social networks are powerful tools that are very attractive to students. Using them as one tool in the classroom could help engage your students and meet many of them where they are already most comfortable.

Other Tools

There are many other tools, and new tools are created all time. Some of them are similar to others just described, and some don't fit into any of the categories. Shared calendar tools like 30 Boxes (www.30boxes.com) and Google Calendar (http://calendar.google.com) make it easy to share calendars. Doodle (www.doodle.com) helps you set up a meeting with others by providing possible times for individuals to enter when they are available. SurveyMonkey (www.surveymonkey.com) and Polldaddy (http://polldaddy.com) allow you to create online surveys. Many quiz sites, such as QuizRevolution (www.quizrevolution.com) allow you to create online quizzes. Copia (www.thecopia.com) is a site that combines several different ideas. It merges electronic books (e-books) with social networking, allowing you to read a book and share your comments with others. Comments can show up right in the book. This could be a powerful application for schools that want to move to e-books. Glogster (http://edu.glogster.com) is a tool for creation of interactive posters. Museum Box (http://museumbox.e2bn.org) is a tool for creating a virtual multimedia museum display case. Prezi (http://prezi.com) is online presentation software. Similar to an online version of PowerPoint, its presentation model is very different (go try it to see what I mean). There are many more. Visit Cool Tools for Schools (http://cooltoolsforschools.wikispaces.com) or start building your own personal learning network to learn about new tools as they come out.

RSS

Now that it is so easy to share information with others, you might be overwhelmed. Your friends, teachers, students, colleagues, relatives, neighbors, and grocery stores are sharing all the time. How can you keep up with it all?

WEB FEED STANDARDS

RSS is a specific form of web feed. RSS is the most well-known and widely used format for subscribing to web pages, but it is not the only one. Atom (www.atom.com) is a competing standard that was developed around 2003. Atom has been incorporated into many feed tools, such as Google Reader, but it has not been as widely accepted as RSS. Because *RSS* is a more widely used term than *web feed* and because RSS is more widely used than any other form of web feed, I will use the term *RSS*, and you shouldn't worry if you are subscribing to sources that use RSS or Atom or something else.

You can't possibly visit 50 blogs, 23 social bookmarks pages, 15 wikis, ad infinitum. And the worst part is, if you were to go to 50 blogs, you'd find out 47 of them don't have anything new for you to read. Wouldn't it be nice if there were a way for you to be informed of what's new in your personal learning network in one place? The answer is RSS (Really Simple Syndication).

As a consumer of information, you will be interested in RSS as way to keep up with everything that interests you by subscribing to web pages. As a producer of information, you will be interested in RSS as a way for others to keep up with the information you create. If you create web pages and want to include an RSS feed on your page, you can find some XML code to add to your site, but fortunately, it is much easier than that. Many of the Web 2.0 tools we have discussed have RSS feeds built-in. If you create a blog or a wiki, you don't have to do anything to create the feed. Others will be able to subscribe automatically.

If you see the symbol below (Figure 5.1) in the address bar of your browser (or the command bar in Internet Explorer), you can click on it to subscribe to the feed (note that some browsers use different symbols to indicate that the page can be subscribed to). But first, you need to set up your feed reader. Some browsers and email systems have them built-in, or you can use a downloadable tool or a feed system, like Google Reader. (For Google Reader, you need to have a Google account.)

Figure 5.1 This is an RSS feed icon.

Find a blog that interests you and click on the feed icon (Figure 5.1). If you don't know where to start, you might try David Warlick's blog (http://davidwarlick.com/2cents) or Will Richardson's blog (http://willrichardson.com), two interesting blogs about educational technology and education reform. If you just subscribe to one or two things, it might not make sense to subscribe at all. Just go to your one or two favorite places each day to check for updates. However, if you have more than two, a tool like Google Reader will give you a one-stop shop for anything that interests you. If there is anything new at any of those sites, it will let you know and save time.

To give examples of the kinds of things to which you can subscribe, I'll tell you some of the things I subscribe to besides Educational Technology blogs such as those of David Warlick and Will Richardson. In addition to being a pointy-headed intellectual in an ivory tower, I am a sports fan, so I subscribe to feeds about my favorite teams. Some of the feeds are for the sports section of specific newspapers, such as the football section of the Miami Herald (www.miamiherald.com/sports/football) and the Yahoo page about a specific team, such as the University of Illinois football page (http://rivals.yahoo.com/ncaa/football/teams/iic). I also enjoy reading several columnists from the *New York Times*, such as Tom Friedman (http://topics.nytimes.com/top/opinion/editorialsandoped/oped/columnists/thomaslfriedman). My wife is a chocolatier, so I subscribe to her business blog (http://trufflesbyemily.blogspot.com) to keep up with her professional accomplishments and give her a plug—otherwise, she won't let me sample her truffles. I make my students blog for one of my classes, so I subscribe to their blogs (at least until the course is over). Because my last book was about PowerPoint, I spend a lot of time answering PowerPoint questions and subscribe to the PowerPoint forums (e.g., http://answers.microsoft.com/en-us/office/forum/powerpoint) to find out when a new question has been asked. A friend just turned her minivan into an art car and has been blogging about it (http://joans-art-car.blogspot.com).

My colleagues and I have been blogging together about uses of iPads in education (http://ipadloyola.blogspot.com), so I subscribe to that to make sure my posts went through and to see if anyone else has posted. I have been working on a chapter for another book that is a large, collaborative effort (several different people wrote chapters). The editors set up a wiki for information about the progress of the book, so I subscribe to that to make sure I don't miss an announcement about a new deadline. I also have some news searches set up in Google News. If you're interested in following the news about a particular topic, go to Google News (http://news.google.com) and search for that topic. The search results will have a feed icon so you can subscribe to that search. When a new news story comes out about that topic, it will show up in your RSS reader.

■ GETTING A GOOGLE READER ACCOUNT

A Google account is needed for Google Reader. Do you have one? If you don't have one by now, you haven't been playing with enough of the tools in this book! It's simple. Go to http://reader.google.com to create one.

If you subscribe the way I do, you will get hundreds of messages a day. Just look for the "Mark all as read" button. Subscribing to something isn't a commitment to read it. I might get 50 messages about environmental topics that interest me. I scan the headlines, click on one or two, and mark the rest as read without giving it a second thought. RSS is there to help you aggregate what you want, not to overwhelm you with tons of useless junk.

Next, you might decide that what you really want is to collect items for your students to read. Instead of using Google Reader, you might use a tool like Netvibes (www.netvibes. com) to create pages around topics and gather together information from various sources. Netvibes includes many widgets, such as weather, as well as the ability to add RSS feeds. You might decide to make available to your class a list of the latest blog postings around a particular topic. You can search out the blogs, put them on a Netvibes tab, and share that tab publicly. Now, you just have to direct your students to that tab. Here is an example from Jeremy Sands, a journalism teacher at Stone Ridge School of the Sacred Heart: www.netvibes.com/mr-sands#Journalism_Resources. Note that this particular tab is public and available to everyone, including his journalism students, but the rest of his tabs are private, so he can put all his nonschool-related links there as well.

Safety and Web 2.0

Web 2.0 provides a number of challenges to safety. That is why many school systems block Web 2.0 tools. I believe that they can be used under the supervision of a teacher to do great things in the classroom. However, this requires precautions. The main issues have to do with inappropriate content and inappropriate contact. Because Web 2.0 makes it easy for people to put things on the web, some of the material in Web 2.0 applications can be inappropriate for students. Many educators love to have their students make glogs—interactive multimedia images that look like posters (see www.glogster. com)—because it is easy to make an online poster, but not all glogs are educational or without inappropriate material. Additionally, Web 2.0 allows contact with people outside the classroom, and that contact might not always be appropriate.

Teachers need to take precautions.

1. **Educate yourself about the Web 2.0 tool you are using.** Find out if it is locked down for educational uses only or if it is open to the public, and understand the potential for inappropriate material on the site.

2. **Inform parents.** Parents don't like to be surprised. Make it clear to parents what tools you are using, what risks those tools pose, what supervision they might need to provide for students using the tools at home, and, most important, what educational benefits the tools provide.

3. **Follow normal safety precautions and school rules.** For example, many schools require that students only use first names online and never post personal information such as phone numbers and addresses.

4. **Educate students about appropriate behavior,** including what to do when they find inappropriate content online.

5. **Take advantage of features of the tools that let you monitor and/or moderate what gets put online** so you will know right away if outsiders are making inappropriate contact.

A few simple precautions can go a long way so you can take advantage of the power of the web and Web 2.0 with your students. There are risks, but the risks of not educating our students in 21st-century learning environments are even greater.

Cloud Computing and Web 2.0

Do you feel safe having everything you use stored locally on your own computer? It's only a little safer than keeping all of your money under your mattress. As time has gone on, society has gotten more and more comfortable offloading many things to the "cloud." That is, a lot of our stuff is "out there" somewhere. This is hard when you are talking about property and physical stuff, but the things we deal with on our computer are all virtual; they are just a bunch of 1s and 0s. It is not a great leap to jump from having them sitting on our hard drives, where we can't really touch them or feel them, to having them sitting in a server farm in Colorado (or Idaho or California or China). In fact, since the only way we can touch them or feel them is through a mouse, keyboard, and screen, we can actually touch them and feel them more when they are in Colorado. We can access them from our home computers, cell phones, work computers, iPads, friends' computers, Internet cafés, and so on.

Until recently, the cloud was mostly about storing our data. We could have virtual hard drives to keep stuff somewhere else, such as Dropbox (http://dropbox.com) and Google Drive (http://drive.google.com). We would still use the power of our own computers to run programs or applications to access and manipulate our stuff. This provides security, backups, and easier access to our data from a variety of locations. But why do we need the applications on our drives at all? As networks have become faster, it has become reasonable to let the server in Colorado store our data *and* run our applications.

This cloud concept has been around for many years (actually before PCs were common), known as *thin client computing*. The basic idea is that your computer is mainly a dumb terminal, and a computer or computers elsewhere process the information and put it on your screen. You don't need a powerful computer because your computer isn't doing much computing. Originally, with thin client computing, you generally accessed a dedicated server, often one very close by. I access some applications via Citrix, which runs off a server in my school. With cloud computing, as the term *cloud* implies, you are accessing some amorphous thing out there somewhere. In fact, you might be accessing a dedicated server for your school or school system, but you might be accessing a number of different servers spread around the country or the world. When everything goes well, you won't even notice the difference, and you won't care where the processing is taking place.

Some of the major players in cloud computing are Google, Microsoft, and Citrix. Google has developed Google Docs, which includes word processing, spreadsheets, presentations, drawing, and forms (and by the time this book is published, probably three more things). With the latest version of Microsoft Office and Windows, Microsoft has introduced versions of Office applications online (see, for example, their To the Cloud commercials: www.microsoft.com/en-us/showcase/details.aspx?uuid=8f01d2e5-0c99-4780-9d1d-e40000179b0e; see also Cloud on Your Terms: www.microsoft.com/en-us/showcase/details.aspx?uuid=e3848127-3dd6-473a-9ea5-24960520a83b).

Citrix is generally more of a traditional thin-client system that allows schools to put full versions of applications on a server for easy access.

One of the disadvantages of cloud computing is that most cloud applications are not as powerful as the ones that run locally. If you are a spreadsheet guru, you will not be happy with the current spreadsheet in Google Docs, for example. But if you just want to make some simple spreadsheets, Google Docs is great.

The advantages of cloud computing are numerous. You have access to your applications and your data from any networked computer. Sharing and collaboration becomes much easier (store a document on Google Docs and invite contributors, and you suddenly have a collaborative workspace). As the cloud applications improve, you do not have to upgrade your software. Additionally, many cloud applications tend to be cheap or even free. Finally, technology support can be reduced or redirected because you don't have to install upgrades or the original programs.

So with easier maintenance and anytime-anywhere access to your stuff, why wouldn't you want to be in the cloud for everything? The two biggest issues for schools with cloud computing will be bandwidth and security. The more you do in the cloud, the more bandwidth you will need to move information around. If you're doing spreadsheets, file sizes are small, but if you're doing digital video editing, you can easily clog your network.

Security is a big issue for schools. Schools simply cannot store sensitive data on clouds that don't follow the Family Educational Rights and Privacy Act (FERPA) guidelines (see www2.ed.gov/policy/gen/guid/fpco/ferpa). Many companies do provide cloud-based grade book solutions that follow FERPA guidelines, but if you want to keep your grades on a random, online spreadsheet, be careful that you are not violating FERPA. However, for nonsensitive data, this is not a problem, though many schools and individuals find the privacy policies of cloud services, such as Google Docs, to be troubling and avoid using them altogether.

One last disadvantage and one last advantage: change and sharing. Applications in the cloud can and do change regularly. Companies go out of business (many companies that provide cloud applications don't have a firm business model with an easy source of revenue), so applications can go away without notice. Further, the cloud keeps you from having to worry about managing upgrades, but it also removes the power to manage upgrades. Many of us recently went through the process of upgrading from Microsoft Office 2003 to 2007 (for those of you haven't done this, just note that Office changed significantly from 2003 to 2007). I hope you had some advance warning about this and received some training to prepare you. Now, imagine your application was in the cloud, and you showed up one day to a totally new interface. That can happen in the cloud. Most changes are simply tweaks to the earlier version, but in the cloud you have no control. If the creator of the program makes a change (like Facebook's timeline), you are stuck with it. You can't even keep a copy of the 2003 version on your computer because the 2003 version never resided on your computer.

Finally: there are advantages in sharing. When your stuff is in the cloud, it is not only accessible to you wherever you want it. It is accessible to anyone you want to give access to it. Change your mindset from "this document is mine unless I share it" to "this document is shared unless I protect it." The cloud makes sharing natural and easy. It doesn't require collaboration, but it streamlines collaboration. Sometimes making something slightly easier is all it takes for it to tip (Marcovitz, 2009) and become a widely used practice.

By its ease of use, low cost, and ease of collaboration, cloud computing can be a powerful tool for educators.

You might be asking yourself what the difference is between cloud computing and Web 2.0. The answer is not much. Because there are no strict definitions of either, there is no clear distinction and no need to decide whether something is one or the other or both. Both cloud computing and Web 2.0 make computing power available on the web and add to the ease of sharing on the web. One distinction is that cloud computing is a more coordinated effort than Web 2.0. In a way, you make a decision to move "to the cloud" by investing in resources that are only available online, while Web 2.0 is a series of unrelated tools that come and go from your use (or even existence) and are easily used and discarded. However, don't worry about the distinctions. You might even notice that I've mentioned Google Docs in both sections. Your goal is to find tools that you can use. If you are looking for institutional solutions for your school or district, you are probably using the term *cloud computing,* but if you are looking for individual solutions for yourself or other teachers, you are probably using the term *Web 2.0.* But you might be talking about the same tool.

Conclusion

Web 2.0 is about easy-to-use tools that can help you and your students become participants in the web, not spectators. Web 1.0, for most people, was about consuming information. Web 2.0 is about consuming, producing, and interacting. It's about building communities, sharing ideas, learning from others, and teaching others. It's not about the tools themselves; it's about finding tools that help you do what you want to do.

Some classrooms are built entirely around one tool, such as blogs, but digital-age learners learn to use the available tools to solve real problems. They jump around from tool to tool as needed, incorporating new tools all the time and jettisoning old ones that are no longer popular or useful. Certainly, you want to start with one or two easy tools until you feel comfortable, but most of the tools are easy enough to incorporate with very little work. You want to get wedded to your learning outcomes and goals, not the tools. If a tool makes it easier for your students to learn, use it. If it doesn't, use something else. Don't think about whether you want to use a blog or a wiki. Think about whether you want to make connections outside your classroom. Think about whether you want authentic audiences. Think about whether you want to share your own thoughts with your students and others. Think about whether you want to encourage collaborative work. In other words, think about your goals, not your tools. Then, look for tools that help you achieve your goals. Chances are, you'll find easy Web 2.0 tools that can help you and your students learn in several new, exciting ways.

Exercises

1. Create a blog about any topic that interests you personally or professionally. Try to write something in it at least once per week, and try to have most of your entries link to other information on the web that you analyze in your blog.

2. Pick five tools listed in this chapter (or at one of the sites listed in this chapter), create accounts for them, and create something to test out those tools. Bonus: think about how you might use each tool in your classroom, and write about what you find in your blog.

3. Pick something in your curriculum that might benefit from online, collaborative tools. This might be something that works fairly well in your classroom now, something you struggle with, or something that you haven't been able to do at all. Find two or more Web 2.0 tools that might help you with that curricular goal. Play with the tools and develop a lesson plan. Bonus: put the lesson plan online to share with others.

4. Develop a personal learning network by finding at least 10 sources of information and subscribing to them in an RSS reader.

References

Bergmann, J., & Sams, A. (2012). *Flip your classroom: Reach every student in every class every day.* Eugene, OR: International Society for Technology in Education.

Burbules, N. C., & Callister, T. A., Jr. (2000). *Watch IT: The risks and promises of information technologies for education.* Boulder, CO: Westview Press.

Cain, J. (2007, January 3). Podcasting enables 24/7 foreign language study. *MIT News.* Retrieved January 4, 2012, from http://web.mit.edu/newsoffice/2007/podcasting-fll.html

Cuban, L. (1986). *Teachers and machines: The classroom use of technology since 1920.* New York, NY: Teachers College Press.

Fanuko, K. (2010, November 22). Tinley teacher turns social media into tools. Southtown Star. Retrieved from http://southtownstar.suntimes.com/photos/galleries/2672191-417/students-moore-book-class-social.htm

Marcovitz, D. M. (2006). Changing schools with technology: What every school should know about innovation. In R. C. Hunter (Series Ed.) & S. Y. Tettegah (Vol. Ed.), *Advances in educational administration, Vol. 8: Technology and education: Issues in administration, policy, and applications in K12 schools* (pp. 3–15). London, UK: Elsevier.

Marcovitz, D. M. (2009, March). *Educational technology and the tipping point.* Paper presented at the Society for Information Technology and Teacher Education 2009 Conference, Charleston, SC.

Richardson, W. (2010). *Blogs, wikis, podcasts, and other powerful web tools for classrooms.* Thousand Oaks, CA: Corwin.

Rosenberg, S. (2010, September 2). In defense of links, part three: In links we trust [Blog post]. Retrieved from http://www.wordyard.com/2010/09/02in-defense-of-links-part-three-in-links-we-trust

Suziea. (Vesper, S.) (2007, July 17). A new way to publish—The rise of Web 2.0. Retrieved January 11, 2011, from http://www1.teachertube.com/viewVideo.php?video_id=4089&title=A_New_Way_to_Publish___The_Rise_of_Web_2_0

Vincent, T. (2009) *Podcasting for teachers and students.* Phoenix, AZ: tony@learninginhand.com. Available from http://learninginhand.com/storage/podcasting_images/Podcasting_Booklet.pdf

CHAPTER SIX

Searching the Web

Laverty, Reed, and Lee (2008) researched the web literacy of teacher candidates:

> Teachers need the skills to locate these tools on the web and also the ability to teach their students web search and evaluation strategies so that students can effectively explore the web by themselves. Conversely, Google's "I'm Feeling Lucky" button suggests that a single query can be answered by a single website and epitomizes the notion that web searching is easy. The physical design of a single box on a blank page reinforces the idea that a few words can retrieve specific information. This is actually the converse of what happens in practice. Satisfactory results may be found quickly when topics are straightforward. For complex ideas, however, the single search box masks the depth and abundance of information that is potentially accessible. It creates the illusion that deep thinking is not necessary to penetrate the expression of sophisticated ideas. The reality of web searching is that far more skill is needed for narrowly focused returns. (para. 2)

Searching the web is easy. Just go to your favorite search engine and type a word or phrase, and the results come flowing. For most of what you want to do, that works just fine. Chapter Two, Critical Information Literacy, discusses why you might want to apply more critical thinking skills to your searches and what you find. This chapter helps you use your search tools more effectively, whether you are reading as a dialectical reader or just searching for something a little out of the ordinary.

Searching Is Easy … or Is It?

What two historical documents were linked from the main White House web page in October 1997? I'll wait while you go search for that. … I'm still waiting. … You might have come across a class agenda where I ask this question, but you will not easily find the answer. After about fifteen minutes, fewer than 5% of my graduate students (mostly teachers in an educational technology program) could find the answer. Did you get the *National Enquirer* and Bill Clinton's resignation? You would be wrong if you did, but that's the answer given on Yahoo! Answers. (The correct answers are at the end of this chapter.)

This is an example of the kind of question that Google or Bing or any other search engine has a hard time finding. In fact, it is possible that you would never find the answer with a regular search engine. Let's try another question.

What is the most popular type of milk in the United States? I was at the store with my daughter Ella (I think she was 11 at the time), and we needed milk. Because this wasn't a grocery store, but a store that happened to have a small grocery section, it didn't have a wide range of choices for milk. My daughter was shocked that they didn't have any 1% milk. She protested, "That is the most popular type of milk. Why wouldn't they have it?" I suggested that it was the most popular type of milk in the Marcovitz household, but I didn't know what the most popular type of milk was in the rest of the country. I guessed it wasn't 1% because, if it were, the store would have carried it. Answering this question proved to be harder than I anticipated. Like most of you, I was sure that I could find just about anything by using Google. I think it took me about 15 minutes. Unlike the first question, this is very findable with Google; it's just not easy.

Those are my two questions to get people to realize that searching isn't always easy. Because a simple search works so often, many people never improve their skills beyond knowing the address of their favorite search engine. In case you're ready to go beyond simple searches, the rest of this chapter will describe a few pointers to help you and to help your students search more effectively.

What's Not on the Web?

Joyce Valenza (2001) asked this question in 2001. Over a decade ago, the answer was that there was a lot of stuff that wasn't on the web. More things are on the web today, but many still aren't. Valenza's first concern was that students were missing things that could be found in perfectly good books because they opted for brief, shallow summaries from the web. She used the example of a paper by a student about Hitler that had many holes because the student never looked at the biography of Hitler or his own writing, *Mein Kampf*, on the library shelves. Another example took a student to the *Reader's Guide to Periodicals* when searching information about breakdancing to find that many articles were written about it in *Time* magazine in the late 1980s. If Valenza's article were written today, it would need new examples because *Mein Kampf* is easily found at Project Gutenberg (http://gutenberg.net.au/ebooks02/0200601.txt), as is the complete archive of *Time* (http://search.time.com/results.html), though to read entire articles you must be a subscriber to the magazine. It is true that many books and articles are not available for free on the web. Valenza uses the example of finding great pictures from Mathew B. Brady of the Civil War but missing the material in Bruce Catton's book, *The Civil War*. With Google books (http://books.google.com), the first 77 pages of Catton's book are free for viewing, but the entire book is only available online by purchasing it. Many journals and magazines appear on the web, and many others are hidden in databases that can only be accessed through the library. Valenza's article, for example, was available to me through the Academic OneFile database (http://find.galegroup.com/gtx/start.do?prodId=AONE) purchased by my library but not available for free without affiliation with a library that purchased it (see Figure 6.1).

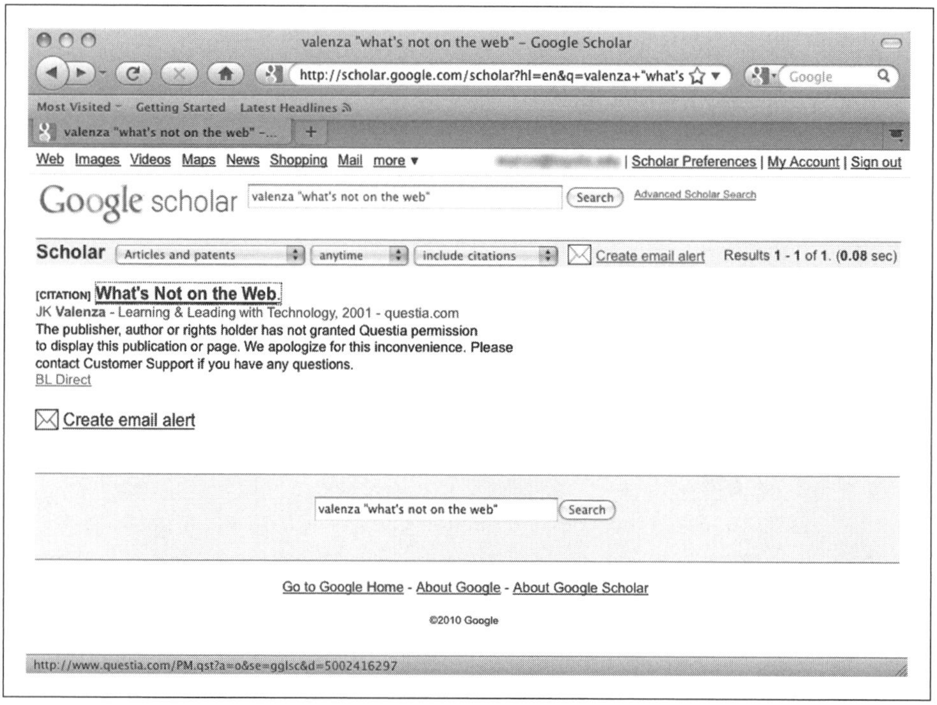

Figure 6.1 Google Scholar search for Valenza, "What's Not on the Web?"

Although many more things are available online for free, Valenza's (2001) list still holds true. She says that on the web, students won't find many high-quality reference books, full-text nonfiction, any book that is still covered by copyright, comprehensive periodical indexes, or magazine articles written before 1990. Although more of this material is available for free today, much of it still requires access to a good library.

Searching Strategies

You want to find information about peanuts. What do you do? If you're like most of your students (or most anyone), you'll type the word *peanuts* into your search engine. What you'll find is a wide range of sites about buying peanuts, Snoopy, peanut brittle, and so on. The first step might be asking a better question and refining what you want to know. For example, if you want information about growing peanuts, you might type *growing peanuts* into your search engine. Many times a simple refinement like that makes the search much better.

Sometimes you know what you don't want better than you know what you want. For our peanut search, you might know, for example, that you don't want any information about the Snoopy (Charlie Brown, Lucy, et al.) comic strip. Therefore, you might type *peanuts -Snoopy* (that is, *peanuts* with a hyphen/minus sign before *Snoopy*) into your search engine to say you want *peanuts* and not *Snoopy*.

Search engines have gotten pretty good about finding results based on the words you type and the order you type them, so if you search for *civil war,* you are likely to get results about the Civil War, not just a bunch of pages that contain the words *civil* and *war*. However, sometimes you want to find an exact phrase. In that case, putting quotes around the phrase (e.g., *"civil war"*) helps the search engine know that you want the exact phrase.

The Boolean operator *OR* can help if you are looking for more than one possibility. If you can't remember whether your favorite page about searching strategies was written by Marcovitz or Valenza, you might try *"searching strategies" marcovitz OR valenza* for your search.

Sometimes it is difficult to remember exactly which tricks work in which search engine—in Google, for example, not capitalizing the *OR* gives different results—or other tricks that might be useful. In that case, you might want to look for advanced search options. These can be found by performing a regular search and then clicking on the Options button (it looks like a gear in the top right of the screen) and choosing "Advanced search." This provides a fill-in form for the above options as well as many others. My favorite search strategy is usage rights (see Chapter Seven for more about this). Other favorites are to narrow the search by date, so I can look for pages that were written or updated recently, and select "Find pages that link to the page." This is also available by putting the word *link* followed by a colon (*link:*) before a URL in the search engine to find out what pages link to a particular website. A new option from Google also allows you to choose basic, intermediate, or advanced for reading level.

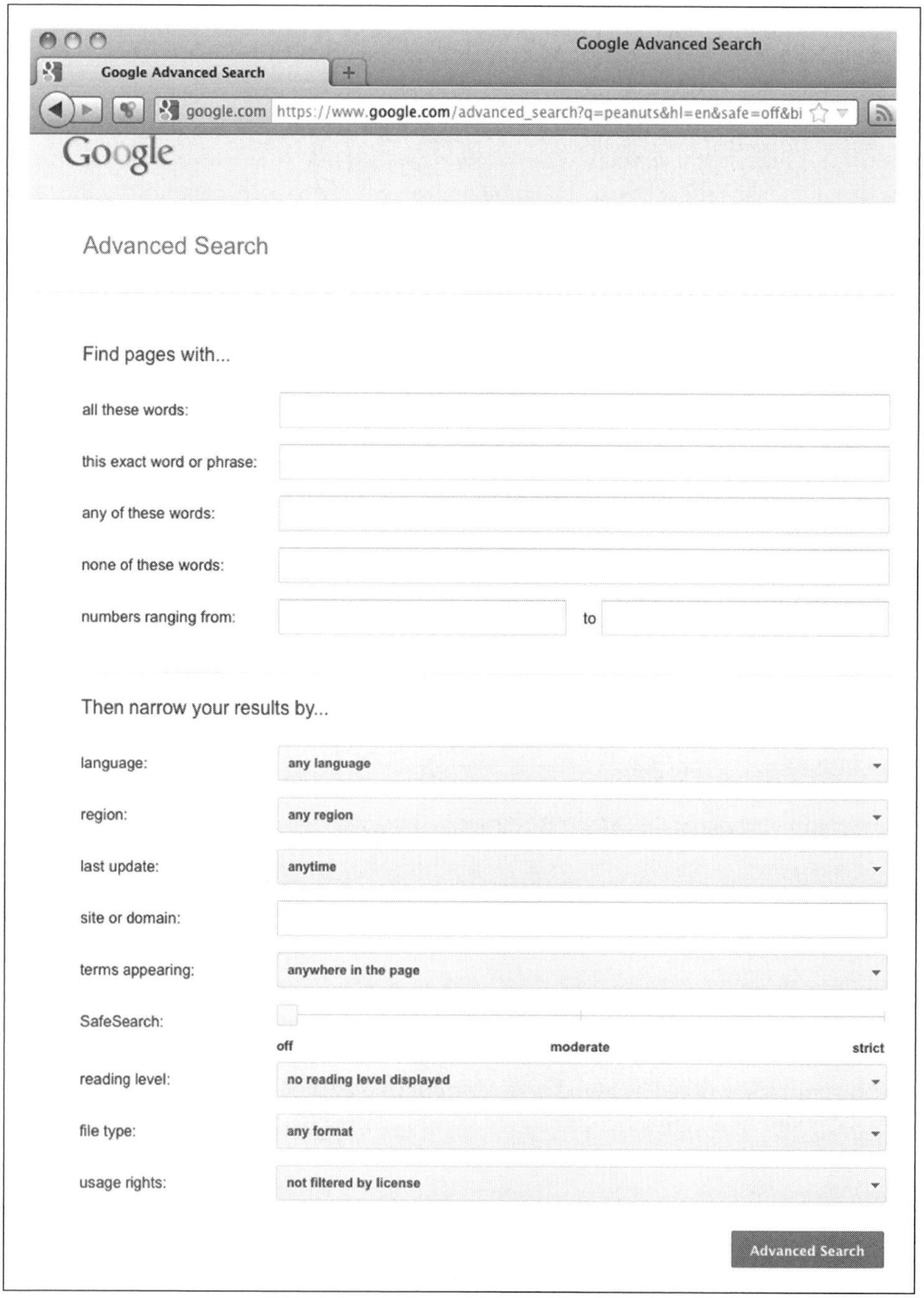

Figure 6.2 Advanced Search in Google.

Figure 6.2 shows an advanced search. This won't help you narrow down between sites for second graders and sites for fifth graders, but it can, at least, cut out results that require a college degree to understand.

Ask the Right Questions

Search tools and tips can be helpful, but Elliot Soloway (Leibovich, 2000) recommends asking better questions and avoiding Boolean logic. He suggests phrasing the search in the form of a question, picking out the key words and other important words related to the question, and typing a few of those words into the search engine. This simple step will help students immediately focus on what is important, rather than quotation marks and other codes for the search engine. Soloway recommends trying the search again in a separate browser window with the words in a different order and looking at what results are in common from the first couple of pages of search results. He also suggests that you find five pages, copy the URLs to a word processor document, and type annotations for each site. If you haven't found the answer yet, work on the question and try again with new key words.

Some searches fail because the information you want isn't available. Other searches fail because you haven't asked the right question. An exercise like this will help you refine your question until you ask the best possible question.

Search Tools

Most people have their favorite search engines and go to them for all their searching needs. The most popular are Google (www.google.com), Bing (www.bing.com), and Yahoo! (www.yahoo.com). Because these tools are in competition with each other, they are constantly improving. Some of the improvements are attempts to get better results, and some are to make it easier to wade through the pages of results you get. Others are to add new tools. Here is a selection of tools that you won't find by doing a simple Google, Bing, or Yahoo! search.

Clustered Results, Clustering Tools

Yippy (http://www.yippy.com) looks like a regular search engine, but it adds a feature to cluster the top results into clouds that categorize the results, sometimes in intelligent ways and sometimes not. Let's look at our *peanuts* search from earlier. We can use some of the strategies mentioned above to try to eliminate results for Snoopy. Alternatively, we can go to Yippy and see the following clouds: Comic Strip (30), Nuts (31), Peanut butter (26), Grow (20), Brittle (13), Virginia (11), Boiled (9), Raw Shelled (9), Eat (7), Ground (6). The numbers of hits from the top 193 results are listed in parentheses and a "more" button provides another 19 clouds. Other clustering tools include WebClust (http://www.webclust.com) and iBoogie (http://clusteredsearch.com).

Metasearches

Dogpile (http://www.dogpile.com) does not have its own search database. Instead it searches the results from other search engines. When the web was new, different search engines would get vastly different results, and the best search engines would only find about 16% of what was available on the web (Introna & Nissenbaum, 2000). Now, search engines are better, but, sometimes, it helps to search for the same thing with multiple search engines. Dogpile currently searches Google, Yahoo!, Bing, and Ask. When you get the results, it tells which search engine(s) gave you those results. It also disperses the ads from those sites throughout the results so be careful to look for the word *Sponsored* next to some of the results. Other metasearch engines include, Monster Crawler (http://monstercrawler.com) and Seekky (http://seekky.com).

Box 6.1

Are Librarians Obsolete?

As books become obsolete, you might wonder why we need libraries and librarians at all. The reality is that librarians have never been only interested in books. Librarians are information specialists. They help connect people to the information they need. Almost every library now has several Internet-connected computers and many patrons who don't have a clue. Most of the readers of this book (even before reading this chapter) have pretty good search skills, but even advanced searchers are likely to learn something from a librarian. Librarians deal with people who don't otherwise have access to computers or the Internet. They deal with job seekers who have never used online tools to look for a job, reluctant readers who need book suggestions, and professors who need help finding the right reference material. As the Internet has grown to billions of pages, the information landscape is more complex. It is often easier to access information, but coming up with a million hits from Google doesn't necessarily provide understanding. When trying to understand a complex information landscape, there is no better guide than a librarian.

For our students, this means that we shouldn't simply take them to the library for story time. That's important, but we need to train them that, while the first place to look for something might be Google, libraries and librarians are sometimes better choices.

Image Searches

Google Images (http://images.google.com) provides a search engine
for images. Type in keywords, and you are likely to get millions of
pictures. Chapter Seven, Copyright and the Free Web, discusses
some of the copyright caveats with finding pictures on the web.
Additionally, image searches can lead to inappropriate results even
with seemingly innocuous search terms. In addition to the resources
discussed in Chapter Seven, most search engines (e.g., Bing and
Yahoo!) have image search as an option. Additionally, sites where users
upload their own images can be a source of pictures. See, for example,
Flickr (http://www.flickr.com) and Picasa (http://picasaweb.
google.com).

Blogs

Technorati (http://technorati.com) is a search site dedicated to blogs.
Most search engines will not automatically give results from blogs in
their general searches. If you are looking for experts and non-experts
discussing current topics, you might have better luck searching the
blogs. Google Blogs also offers a search of blogs at http://blogsearch.
google.com.

News

Google News (http://news.google.com) allows you to search recent
news articles from thousands of newspapers, magazines, and news-
related blogs all over the world. You can track what's going on with
a broad topic or look for the latest on an obscure topic. A search of
my old high school just let me know that they won the "In the Click"
seatbelt compliance contest. Most of the other major search engines
provide news search as well.

Books

Amazon (http://www.amazon.com) is one of the best places to search for information about books, and you can even search inside many books. Not to be outdone, Google Books (http://books.google.com) has added the capability to search the contents of books. If you read something in a book and can't remember which one it was, Google Books might find it for you and take you directly to the page where it is.

Figure 6.3 shows the results of searching Google Books for the phrase "try again: answer until it's right" (which appears in my earlier book, *Powerful PowerPoint for Educators*). Google Books allows me to scroll through about 25 pages from the book highlighting the phrase I searched for.

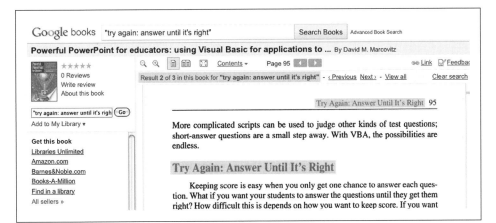

Figure 6.3 Results of a Google Books search for "Try Again: Answer Until It's Right."

Scholarly Articles

Google Scholar (http://scholar.google.com) provides searches through scholarly journals. Some of the articles will be available for free in full text. Other articles require a subscription to a database, something you might be able to access via your school library. This changes the nature of research. If you want high-quality references, including original research, Google Scholar makes it easy to find. Once you find a reference to an article you want, if you can't find it for free online, you can take the reference to your library (either online or in person) and find if it is available to you.

Old Web Pages

The Wayback Machine (http://www.archive.org/web/web.php) at the Internet Archive (http://www.archive.org) allows you to search old versions of web pages. You can use this to find pages that have disappeared from the web or old versions of pages that have changed. Simply type a URL into the Wayback Machine and it will give you a list of dates that are available. For example, to find out what the White House website looked like under previous administrations, simply enter *www.whitehouse.gov* into the Wayback Machine and click on a few of the dates listed. Other than the sneaky question at the beginning of this chapter, I use this quite a bit when I find that articles I want my students to read have disappeared from the web. For example, even though it is not available anywhere else on the free web, you can find my original article from 1997 about critical information literacy at http://web.archive.org/web/20030822105546/www.dayton. isd.esc4.net/tiegrant/tie2modules/tie2readings/marcovitz.pdf.

Charity Searches

GoodSearch (http://www.goodsearch.com) allows you to donate to your favorite charity by searching. Search engines make money by advertising (see Advertising on Searches, later in this chapter). GoodSearch takes some of that revenue and shares it with the charity of your choice. The results are the same as they would be for one of the other popular search engines (currently Yahoo!), but they split the money with your charity and the search company. Although your school is unlikely to make a lot of money from Internet searches, you could designate GoodSearch (or one of the other charity search engines) to be the default search engine on all your computers and set your school to be the charity of choice. Add to school fund-raising possibilities by telling all the students and parents in your school to use GoodSearch as well. Other charity search engines include Search Kindly (http://www.searchkindly.org) and EveryClick (http://www.everyclick.com).

Other Tools

Search engines are in competition with each other so they are adding new tools all the time. Look along the top of the page at Google for other options including the "More" option that lists additional search tools. Bing lists additional tools on the left. Also, think about specialized places that might have better information than a general search. For example, you might search the Better Business Bureau database (http://www.bbb.org/us/Find-Business-Reviews) to find out if a business is reputable, or you might search Edmunds (http://www.edmunds.com) for information about cars.

Child-Friendly Searching

Some schools have policies that young children are not allowed to search. Instead, they must pick from a list of URLs provided by the teacher. This can be good for safety and efficiency, but I do not recommend it as a general policy. It certainly limits (but does not prevent) students from going to inappropriate sites that are either troubling in general or simply off topic. It also keeps students from wasting time by searching inefficiently for information that you can easily provide for them. However, at an early age, students should have some experience finding their own information, even if they are not ready for advanced lessons about critical information literacy (see Chapter Two).

If you allow students to search, you might choose to use a filtered search. Yahoo! Kids (http://kids.yahoo.com) and Ask Kids (www.askkids.com) provide filtered results. Try, for example, typing *sex* into either search engine, and you get no results. This, of course, raises the same issues as filters in general (see Chapter Eight). For some populations and in some contexts, appropriate information about sex should be made available, whether it is about basic human biology or how to determine the sex of a frog. Although these filtered searches can block far too much, they are a good way for younger students to experience searching with limited risks. Additionally, the results are generally geared to children, so the reading level, as well as the content, is more likely to be appropriate.

Google also offers filtered searches when a parent or teacher checks "strict" or "moderate" in the SafeSearch section of settings (Figure 6.4). For more about safety options in Google, see www.google.com/familysafety. Google's SafeSearch is far less restrictive than Yahoo! Kids (http://kids.yahoo.com) or Ask Kids (www.askkids.com), so you should check the results you get before relying on it to block all inappropriate sites. If you like Google's SafeSearch, you can set your default search engine to OneKey (http://onekey.com), which uses Google's SafeSearch to perform its searches. As usual, filtered search engines are not a substitute for appropriate supervision of students.

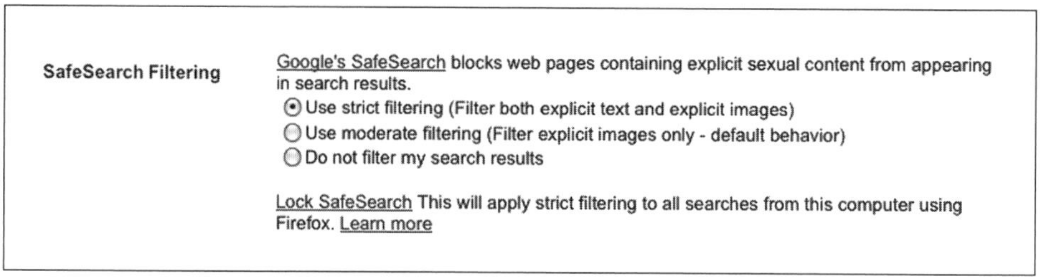

SafeSearch Filtering

Google's SafeSearch blocks web pages containing explicit sexual content from appearing in search results.
- ⦿ Use strict filtering (Filter both explicit text and explicit images)
- ○ Use moderate filtering (Filter explicit images only - default behavior)
- ○ Do not filter my search results

Lock SafeSearch This will apply strict filtering to all searches from this computer using Firefox. Learn more

Figure 6.4 Google SafeSearch settings.

One last searching option for children is KidsClick! (www.kidsclick.org). Most filters attempt to exclude the inappropriate material (in the particular ways they define "inappropriate") from the search results. KidsClick! is a site created by librarians that treats the web like a bookseller for its library. Rather than blocking some sites from the long list of sites, they decide up front what to put on their virtual library shelves and list it along with the reading level of the material. There is no way that a small group of humans can find everything that is good on the web to include, but they continually choose what they can find as the best and most appropriate materials.

Ask a Person

Sometimes the answer you want isn't easily found on the web. This might be a good time to opt for crowdsourcing. Crowdsourcing is used by businesses to get lots of people to submit ideas so they can just pay for the one they choose. It can also be used by individuals to get help or answers. If you have a large following on the web (through Twitter or Facebook, for example), you might ask the people who follow you for help. For example, David Warlick recently asked his 10,000 followers on Twitter (http://twitter.com/dwarlick): "Does anyone know of a simple iPad/iPhone app that will post to Twitter and Facebook? I do not want all Tweets to be copied to Facebook." Pingle (http://itunes.apple.com/us/app/pingle/id303499367?mt=8) was recommended to him by one of his followers. He also regularly asks for ideas for his talks.

If you don't have 10,000 followers, you can try sites like Yahoo! Answers (http://answers.yahoo.com) or WikiAnswers (http://wiki.answers.com), but the results aren't always immediate, and if you can't find it easily with a search, there is a good chance the crowd won't find it either. You might also look to the old-fashioned newsgroup technology. There are still many discussion groups using this technology, which has been around since long before the World Wide Web. Now you can access it by going to Google Groups (http://groups.google.com). You can either search for an answer among the many discussion groups or find a group that is related to the topic of your question and post a question for the group. Some groups are very active and have hundreds or thousands of participants and dozens of posts per day. Other groups are far less active, or defunct, with no one left reading them.

Advertising on Searches

Search engines make their money from advertising. When you search for something, search engines use, in part, the terms you searched for to decide which ads to display. If you search for tires, you are likely to get ads from tire stores. Search engines often keep track of what sites you visit and other information you access to try to make the ads they display more relevant to you. This raises many privacy concerns, and it is a constantly changing landscape, so I encourage you to look for more recent information about this than what you can find in a book like this one. Any specific suggestions I might write now would be outdated by the time this book is printed. You could start by looking at the Electronic Privacy Information Center (http://epic.org).

Ads can be beneficial if you want buy something, but I would only view them as positive if you know what you are viewing is an ad. In a 2005 study, Deborah Fallows, of The Pew Internet & American Life Project, found that users were overconfident about their searching abilities. The following results are included in the report's Summary of Findings in the first few pages (Fallows, 2005): "92% of those who use search engines say they are confident about their searching abilities, with over half of them, 52%, saying they're 'very confident.'" However, only "38% of searchers are aware of a distinction between paid and unpaid results," and "18% of searchers overall (47% of searchers who are aware of the distinction) say they can always tell which results are paid or sponsored and which are not."

Although we can bemoan the ignorance of the American public—after all, that's what grabs the headlines—as teachers, we can use this as a teaching opportunity. If we never let our students search, we never give them the opportunity to see the distinction between paid and unpaid results. Search engines are not always very good at making the distinction clear. Google generally highlights the ads at the top of the page and presents a list of clearly marked "Ads" on the right. Bing calls them "Sponsored sites" and lists them on the right. Yahoo! calls them "Sponsored Results" and has a similar layout to Google's. Ask includes some "Sponsored Results" in the middle of the search as a highlighted block. However, the highlighting is in light blue and barely distinguishable from the white background. Dogpile (the metasearch engine) is among the most confusing, as the paid and unpaid results are laid out nearly identically. The difference is that after the URL, an unpaid result will list "Found on" followed by the search engines that gave the result, while a paid result is labeled as "Sponsored" followed by the source of the ad.

If you are interested in opinions about advertising in schools, I encourage you to check out the Alliance for Childhood (allianceforchildhood.org) and the

Center for Commercial-Free Public Education (www.ibiblio.org/commercialfree—the Center is now defunct, but it still has links to many good resources). However, without throwing away computers in schools altogether, the battle to eliminate commercialism from computer use in school is mostly lost. What we can do is make sure our students are educated. At a minimum, we should teach them to distinguish between paid and unpaid search results. Then, as part of a critical information literacy curriculum, we can teach them why paid results might be inappropriate resources, giving biased results.

Box 6.2

How Does a Search Work?

There are billions of web pages. When you type a term into a search engine, it gives you back a list of sites in a matter of seconds (usually less than a second). How does it do that? It clearly does not go out and search each page as you type your question. Instead, search engines have automatic processes, called bots, which are constantly going around the web and indexing pages. They might come to a page and add all the words or phrases on that page to their index and then follow all the links on that page and do the same to those linked pages. Thus, the search engines maintain a giant database of everything that they find on the web. When a new page is added or a page changes, the search engines won't know about it instantly, but over time, they are likely to get back around to that page and update their index for that page. This still requires a tremendous amount of computing power, but not nearly as much as would be required to search the web, rather than their own index, each time a search is performed. Each search engine has its own algorithm for deciding which results to list on top. For example, Google not only looks at how many words you type appear on the web page, but it also looks at how many sites and how many high-quality sites link to the web page. How they define *high quality,* as well as other factors that help them rank pages, is a company secret. Just remember, the search engine's idea of a good site might not match your idea of a good site, so what you're looking for might not be at the top of the list of results.

Conclusion

Most people think that searching is easy. That is because it is … most of the time. Our students won't need advanced search skills for everything they look up. The first hit on Google really does give the right answer a lot of the time. But sometimes it doesn't. Fallows (2005) demonstrates that people are more confident than they should be about their searching capabilities, so it is important that we help our students learn the limitations of a simple Google search and know what to do when the first hit on Google (or the first page of hits) doesn't give us the results we want. This involves helping our students learn how to formulate good questions, sort though the overabundance of results that are given, and find tools beyond Google that might yield better results. This can't be done by ignoring or banning searching. Instead, we need to take some opportunities to help our students become better searchers to help them be better researchers and better thinkers.

Exercises

1. What type of milk (skim, 1%, 2%, or whole) is the most popular milk in the United States? If you have trouble finding this, think about different ways to word your question to narrow down the results. For example, "*milk consumption*" is likely to be more successful than "*milk.*"

2. Think of three of your own questions that can't be easily answered by your students with a Google search.

3. Use some of the search tools and techniques in this chapter to find up-to-date information about privacy and tracking on the web and how searches you make and sites you visit are tracked to change search results as well as ads you see. Write a summary of what is being done to you, what benefits you get from it, and whether you feel the privacy concerns are or are not a problem.

4. Create an assignment for your students to find information that is only partially available online. Give them ideas about how they can use the resources in the library, or other offline resources, to find the complete information.

References

Fallows, D. (2005, January 23). Search engine users. Retrieved December 21, 2010, from Pew Internet & American Life Project, http://www.pewInternet.org/Reports/2005/Search-Engine-Users.aspx

Introna, L., & Nissenbaum, H. (2000). Defining the web: The politics of search engines. *Computer, 33*(1), 54–62.

Laverty, C., Reed, B., & Lee, E. (2008). The "I'm feeling lucky syndrome": Teacher-candidates' knowledge of web searching strategies. *Partnership: The Canadian Journal of Library and Information Practice and Research, 3*(1). Retrieved December 22, 2010, from http://journal.lib.uoguelph.ca/index.php/perj/article/viewArticle/329/892

Leibovich, L. (2000, August 10). Choosing quick hits over the card catalog. *New York Times.* Retrieved December 20, 2010, from http://www.nytimes.com/library/tech/00/08/circuits/articles/10thin.html

Valenza, J. K. (2001). What's not on the web? *Learning & Leading with Technology, 29*(1), 7–9, 48.

Searching Is Easy ... or Is It?

What two historical documents were linked from the main White House web page in October 1997?

If you are still wondering which two historical documents (mentioned on p. 112) were on the White House web page in October 1997, go back and read the Search Tools section under Old Web Pages (p. 122). You can use the Wayback Machine (www.archive.org) to find that the answer is the Declaration of Independence and the Constitution of the United States. (You can also take a historical tour of the White House website starting with Bill Clinton's presidency via the Wayback Machine.)

CHAPTER SEVEN

Copyright and the Free Web

Disclaimer: I am not a lawyer. Any information contained in this chapter is for information purposes only. For important matters of law, contact appropriate legal consultants (your school's or school board's attorney, for example). Also note that this chapter discusses United States copyright law. Most countries have similar laws protecting intellectual property, but laws are different in different countries. For specific information about Creative Commons in countries other than the United States, refer to the Creative Commons website, http://CreativeCommons.org, at the link for Affiliate Network.

The web is full of resources. If you are reading this book, you are looking for ways to use those resources and create your own. Somewhere in the back of your mind, you might be struggling with the idea of copyright and wondering what you are allowed to use and what you are allowed to share. In the age of Web 2.0, where so much personal information is shared on Facebook and YouTube, the concept of copyright might seem to you to be obsolete. From a philosophical perspective, you might be right. As an educator and from a practical perspective, you might be right—at least most of the time. But from a legal and ethical perspective, you would be wrong.

Copyright law intrudes into our online work in two ways. First, it is a problem when gathering information. Because most material on the web is copyrighted, you have limitations when it comes to what you can do with the information you collect. You can certainly read whatever is not locked behind passwords and firewalls, but you might have limits when you want to incorporate that information (especially in its original form) into your own work. Second, it is a problem when distributing information. Although copying something for your class might be OK sometimes, you have far greater restrictions when putting that same material on the web for the whole world to see.

Imagine a world where all creative material that teachers might want to use is locked down. Some things are locked down by law, while others are locked down by technical measures and copy controls. Imagine a world where teachers need permission to use any material they have not created themselves.

Now, imagine a world where teachers have limited rights to use what they want in their teaching. For example, they can show a couple of pictures to their class but not too many. They can create a multimedia project with a short bit of a song, but they can't distribute it too widely or use it for too long. Imagine a world where many things teachers want to do are allowed and many are not, but telling the difference is far from clear.

Finally, imagine a world where teachers can use whatever materials they want in whatever way they want. Imagine a world where pictures, texts, lesson plans, and videos are free for the taking. Imagine a world where teaching materials are widely available for unlimited use.

In reality, we live in all three worlds. The first is the world of copyright law, accompanied by a culture of *no*. The second is the world of fair use, accompanied by a culture of *maybe*. And the third is the world of the commons, accompanied by a culture of *sharing*. This chapter is about navigating these three worlds in education. In a previous publication on copyright, technology, and rights (Marcovitz, 2006), I laid out the basics of copyright law and how educators can take advantage of the fair use provisions of copyright law to use copyrighted material legally with limitations. In this chapter, I expand the discussion of copyright and fair use to include emerging ideas about the commons (see, e.g., Lessig, 2001) and how Creative Commons licensing (see http://creativecommons.org) can help us shift from the world of copyright and fair use to the world of commons and from the culture of *no* and culture of *maybe* to the culture of *sharing.*

This is an important issue in the context of digital communication because the majority of our resources now come from the web, and we are most likely to share these resources on the web. As teachers, we must do this while following legal and ethical principles.

Is Copyright Obsolete?

Lessig (2001) discusses this question from a historical and philosophical perspective. This chapter summarizes some of the history and philosophy and discusses it from a practical perspective. Although rapid changes in technology have gotten well ahead of copyright law, the law still stands, and educators have the moral and legal obligation to follow it. However, the rise in popularity of new mechanisms for copyright permission, primarily Creative Commons, has provided easy access to materials with few or no copyright restrictions. The term *copyleft* (see, e.g., Free Software Foundation, 2009) is often used to refer to mechanisms or licenses that allow the copyright holder to retain some rights while granting broad rights for others to use and share the material.

Imagine that you want to create a digital story with music in the background. Your first inclination might be to remember a popular song that fits the mood of your story perfectly. Then, copyright will surely step in the way. You might remember some obscure rule about only using 30 seconds of the song and another rule imposing limits on how you can distribute your story and for how long. Now imagine that it is not a specific song that you need, but just a type of song that sets the right mood. With that slight change of mindset and a little help from Creative Commons, copyright no longer stands in the way. All you need to do is search for a song that includes appropriate Creative Commons licensing, and you can complete your digital story with few restrictions. Salpeter (2008) and Johnson (2009) give excellent overviews of options within Creative Commons and the importance of Creative Commons for K–12 schools.

Up until a few years ago, Creative Commons was a great idea in theory, but in practice it was largely unusable because of the limited availability of material distributed with Creative Commons licensing. Now, Creative Commons has reached a tipping point. Popular media collections (such as Flickr) and search engines (such as Google) have built-in mechanisms for creators to assign Creative Commons and for users to search for material licensed under Creative Commons. Add to that the Creative Commons website (www.creativecommons.org) and a large supply of media is at the fingertips of every educator. Is everything available that you would ever possibly want to use? Of course not. However, millions of pictures, songs, and videos are freely available.

To answer the question at the beginning of this section, from a practical standpoint, copyright is not obsolete, but with the rise of Creative Commons we are shifting relevance from a culture of copyright to a culture of sharing. The rest of this chapter is divided into three sections: copyright, fair use, and the commons for education.

Copyright and the Culture of *No*

Copyright law was developed to encourage the creation of creative works. By giving creators (such as authors, poets, and photographers) limited rights to control their works, the law builds in incentives to create. For example, if I create something of value, I can copyright it for a period of time so that I can sell it, comfortable with the fact that others do not have the right to copy what I have created and undermine the market for it. For example, I wrote a book in 2004 (second edition, 2012). Although the core of the book was material I had worked on for other purposes and distributed freely on the web, I spent considerable time refining the material into a sellable product. Without the promise of compensation, I would have written some of the material, but I probably would not have expanded it and refined it to the level that I did. In essence, copyright law encouraged me to take the time to expand and polish my work. This benefited me and, I hope, the people who purchased my book. Originally, copyright law gave creators control of their work for 14 years with the option of renewing protection for one additional 14-year period. The current law gives copyright protection to intellectual property until 70 years after the author's death (U.S. Copyright Office, 2009, Chapter 3).

If you want to use my 2004 book or this book, you have several options (aside from waiting for 70 years after I am dead). You can buy the book new in which case I receive royalties. You can buy the book used in which case I receive no royalties. You can borrow the book from a friend or a library (no royalties). The right to give or sell a work to someone else without permission is explicit in Section 109 of the copyright code (U. S. Copyright Office, 2009, Chapter 1, 22–24). Once you have accessed a legal copy, you have limited rights to copy small portions of it for personal use, and you have limited rights to incorporate portions of it in other projects under the fair use provisions found in Section 107 of the copyright code (U. S. Copyright Office, 2009, Chapter 1, 19).

This arrangement works fairly well for content creators who want to control their content. However, it is problematic for users of content. If you want to use content created by someone else, your rights are limited. This is particularly problematic for educators who are simply trying to do their best to teach their students and not trying to make a profit from someone else's work. Fair use (described in more detail in further sections of this chapter) gives educators limited rights to use others' work in their teaching. In some cases, fair use rights are all you need to do what you want. However, the rules are very restrictive when it comes to technology and are complex in general; they don't allow you to distribute others' copyrighted material on the web. The time, portion, and distribution limits for teacher-created multimedia projects are likely to make you not want to use copyrighted material at all. Add to that the complexity of fair use, which is based on case law in applying a four-factor test of "fairness," and you end up with a confusing mess.

This confusion leads to the culture of no (if you are not sure about whether it is legal, just don't use it) or the culture of yes (simply use anything you want for the good of the children). Neither option is reasonable. Teachers should have whatever tools they need to meet the needs of their students, but they must always behave legally and ethically. It is untenable for teachers to stand before their classes and be distributing learning materials in violation of the law.

Why Should I Care about Copyright?

With the laws being so confusing and the chances of being caught so remote, you might wonder why you should care about copyright. You might be thinking, "If I got it from the web, it's already out there, so I should be able to put it on my website." Although this is a convincing argument, it is not the law, it is not ethical, and it is not an appropriate example to set for students. Some sites are supported by advertising, so putting something on your site denies the creator the ad revenue. Other sites might want to attract attention to their products or services for other reasons. Others might want to have the ability to take the material down whenever they want. It is their right, not yours, to control their material. Once you put someone else's work on the web, you have usurped the owner's right.

Legally, you should care about copyright because violations can bring fines of thousands of dollars. Many classroom uses are unlikely to attract attention from the copyright holders or lead to any fines at all, but as material is distributed beyond the classroom walls (including presentations at parent nights, distribution on the web, and distribution for distance learning), the chances of your actions violating the law and being noticed increase greatly.

Ethically, all of us should care about setting a good example for our students. Finding worthwhile material is important, but it should not take place at the expense of setting an example for our students that the law and ethics don't matter. If we show respect for the intellectual property created by writers, artists, and inventors in our classrooms, we'll teach our students the lifelong value of respect for others' work.

Is the Copyright Symbol Necessary?

How many web pages have a copyright symbol? Many do, but many do not. Can you find a copyright symbol on YouTube videos, for example? A copyright notice might take this form:

> © 2012 David M. Marcovitz

That is, it contains the *c* in a circle (or a *p* in a circle for nonvisual material such as sound recordings), the date, and the copyright owner's name, sometimes followed by the phrase "All Rights Reserved." However, a copyright notice is not necessary. As soon as you create a work, you have some copyright protection for that work. If the creator has included the © in the document, that person has thought about protecting it, but even without the copyright symbol, under Unites States law the document is protected. Note that this was enacted as a change to the copyright law in 1989, so some works without a copyright symbol that were created prior to that date might not be protected by copyright law, but you should assume that everything is protected unless you know otherwise.

The copyright holder has the right to seek damages when anyone uses his or her work without getting permission. However, for teachers, our biggest concern is not the prospect of being sued for damages (noncommercial violations of copyright are unlikely to result in large penalties). Our biggest concerns are our obligations as professionals to behave legally and ethically. We must assume that material is copyrighted and that our rights to use it are limited unless we know otherwise.

Public Domain

Exceptions to works being granted automatic copyright relate to the issue of public domain. Works in the public domain are free for anyone to use as they please. Works enter the public domain in three ways:

1. Older works eventually lose their copyright protection and fall into the public domain.

2. Works created by the United States government are automatically in the public domain.

3. The copyright owner may choose to place works in the public domain and forego any copyright protection.

Work is generally copyrighted until 70 years after the death of the author (a recent law extended this from 50 years). Work created by a corporation is generally copyrighted for 95 years after publication (recently extended from 75 years, coincidentally, just in time to save Mickey Mouse from entering the public domain). After the time limits, the work is in the public domain. An author might choose to place his or her work in the public domain. This means that the work can be used by anyone for any purpose. Ethically, you should still give credit to the author, but you may freely use the work.

As educators, this means that we have unlimited rights to use 70-year-old and older works of fiction and nonfiction in any way we choose. Theoretically, we have unlimited rights to use old movies as well, but this doesn't yet apply because most movies are not 95 years old.

Songs present a special case because a song has three potential copyrights: the music, the lyrics, and the performance. Each can be copyrighted separately and may have separate copyright owners. Very old songs might be in the public domain, but the particular recording (i.e., the performance) might not be. If you want unlimited use of old songs, you have to use an old recording or record versions of the songs yourself.

As one final note, public domain grants unlimited rights to use, alter, sell, and copy works. Although you may have no desire to make a profit from the works you create, rather than placing them in the public domain, you might choose to give limited permission, such as for nonprofit educational uses. Creative Commons (www.creativecommons.org) and the Free Software Foundation's public licenses (www.fsf.org) are good models for allowing limited use.

Permission

We know that some things are in the public domain for all to use freely, while other material can be used with limits under fair use (discussed in detail in this chapter's section titled "Fair Use and the Culture of *Maybe*"). Another way to use works created by others is to request and receive permission from the copyright holder. The copyright holder has the right to grant you permission. Sometimes this is easy to obtain, and sometimes it is not. Many copyright holders are sympathetic to nonprofit educational uses and will be happy to give you permission. Other copyright holders, especially for music, lyrics, and works of art, generally charge substantial fees before they will grant anyone permission to reproduce those works.

To request permission, you first must figure out who owns the copyright. This is easy for traditionally published media (such as books, movies, and musical recordings). It will be listed on the copyright page or packaging. Beware when you find something you want to use on the web. Many things are posted on the web by someone other than the copyright holder. Furthermore, the creator isn't necessarily the copyright holder. For many published works, the author retains the copyright. In other cases, the author assigns the copyright to someone else, such as the publisher. In other cases, the copyright might be owned by the employer of the author if the work is considered work for hire. Imagine a greeting card factory where someone is hired to write poems for the inside of greeting cards. Unless the employee and the company make special arrangements, the poems are considered work for hire, and the copyright belongs to the company.

As you create materials, be sure to check with your employer about the arrangements for retaining rights to your own work. In many school systems, teacher-created lessons are owned by the teacher even if they are technically considered work for hire, but that is not universally true.

Once you determine the copyright holder, you can simply send an email or write a letter (assuming you can find contact information on the website where the work was posted). Be clear about exactly how you want to use the material. Copyright holders are unlikely to grant you unlimited permission, but they might be sympathetic to educational uses with limited distribution of the work. Be reasonable and request permission for what you need, not every possible use you might ever want.

Don't be surprised if your request is denied, goes unanswered, or is granted for a fee. Copyright holders have no responsibility to grant you permission, even for your seemingly benign use. Furthermore, they don't even have a responsibility to respond to your request. Many requests for permission include a phrase like, "If I don't hear from you within 30 days, I will assume that permission is granted." Although this is a creative tactic, it will not work. Your assumption of permission is not permission, and failure to respond to such a request is not granting permission. Finally, you might find that copyright holders are willing to grant you permission for a fee. Several years ago, Ann Landers had a very nice column about the failings of computer spell checkers. It was cute, and I wanted to share it with my students, so I wrote to Ann Landers's publisher and requested permission. A quick reply came back, announcing that permission was granted as soon as I sent them a $50 fee. It was cute but not that cute. Instead of distributing the article, I taped it to my office door.

Planning for Copyright

As you plan a project that includes copyrighted material, you must plan for copyright. As you will see following, fair use grants you some rights, but those rights are very limited and often too restrictive. For example, limiting use of a substantial multimedia project to two computers for two years might make the development effort more trouble than it is worth. For that reason, you should plan: plan to get permission, plan for alternatives if permission is not granted, and plan to use as much public domain, copyright-friendly (i.e., work that retains copyright but comes with a notice that many uses are permitted), and self-created material as possible. Seek permission early in the process of designing your project so you still have time to make alternative plans if permission is not granted.

Copyright is good for creators but not always good for users of material. Fortunately, the law has built-in provisions that specify limited rights for what you can use without permission: these limited rights to use copyrighted material are called *fair use*.

Fair Use and the Culture of *Maybe*

Now we know that most written works are copyrighted, and some are in the public domain. We can ask permission to use copyrighted material, and we have the freedom to do what we want with material that is in the public domain. Additionally, we have limited rights to use copyrighted material without asking permission.

Imagine that you are a book author, and you make your living selling books; if you don't sell books, you don't eat. Imagine you are a teacher who finds material online that will benefit your students. Imagine you are a musician who sells millions of albums. Perhaps you are a struggling musician trying to eke a living out of a few album sales and appearances. Imagine you are a librarian trying to disseminate information to the public. Imagine you are a student who found some great pictures on the Internet for a school report.

These examples are just a few of the many competing interests involved in using or limiting the use of information. When I asked my students to role-play some of these roles, they took stands against libraries and used-book sales, in favor of unrestricted use of anything for students and educators, in favor of limiting use to reading books and talking about them, and in favor of a wide range of uses with very strict limitations on the amount of material that may be copied. They learned that copyright laws have to balance these competing interests. Although a bookseller might think it is reasonable that you may not copy even one page from a book, students, teachers, and librarians would find that restriction inappropriate.

The law tries to balance the rights of the copyright holder with the rights of the public, while maintaining its primary goal of promoting the creation of new works, but copyright law is very confusing, especially when applied to the classroom. Many educational applications of copyright law fall under the domain of fair use. This is good and bad. Fair use allows you, as educators, to use material that might otherwise be illegal for you to use. On the other hand, the rules of fair use are complicated and dominated by ambiguous case law. Beware that fair use places limits on the amount of a work (number of words) you may use relative to its entirety (portion limitations); the time for which you may use it (time limitations); and the ways you may distribute it (distribution limitations). These limitations almost certainly prohibit use of any material that is more than a brief quotation when you plan to post it publicly on the web. If you are showing your class a website (or something downloaded from a website), that is generally acceptable, but if you are incorporating it into your own projects or making copies for your class, you will run into time limitations (two years when incorporated into an educational multimedia project and one semester when simply copied), as well as distribution limitations (only loading your educational multimedia project onto two computers at a time for student use). For a complete discussion of fair use and educational multimedia, see Marcovitz (2006) and University of St. Francis (2004).

For educational multimedia, CONFU (the Conference on Fair Use) attempted to form a consensus on fair use in educational multimedia projects (CONFU: The Conference on Fair Use, 1996; Lehman, 1998). CONFU developed guidelines and published them in 1996. However, the participants in CONFU never achieved consensus, with representatives of copyright holders finding the guidelines too permissive and representatives of copyright consumers finding the guidelines too restrictive. With that said, the CONFU guidelines are the best we have. For more details, consult CONFU: The Conference on Fair Use (1996); Davidson (2002); Harper & the University of Texas at Austin (2001, 2007); University of St. Francis (2004); and Lehman (1998). Some of the most common portion limitations include the following:

- Any kind of motion media (movies, videos, etc.) is limited to 10% of the entire work or three minutes, whichever is less.

- Text is limited to 10% of the entire work or 1,000 words, whichever is less.

- Poetry is limited to 250 words. Poems shorter than 250 words may be used in their entirety. Poetry is further limited to use of no more than three poems by one poet or five poems from different poets in an anthology.

- Music, lyrics, and music videos are limited to 10% of the entire work or 30 seconds, whichever is less. Recording your favorite song as the soundtrack of your PowerPoint presentation is not permitted unless it is a very short presentation.

- Pictures and illustrations may be used in their entirety (10% of a picture wouldn't make sense), but no more than five pictures from a single artist and no more than 10% of the images or 15 images, whichever is less, from a collective work may be used.

- Numerical data sets are limited to 10% of the database or 2,500 cell entries, which- ever is less. Note that cell entries refer to individual pieces of information, such as a name or a website's URL.

These limitations are fairly restrictive. You may not post copyrighted work on your website. You may not make CDs and distribute your work to your entire class. You may not use the copyrighted work for commercial or noncurricular uses, so you may not use clips of popular songs (even if they are each less than 30 seconds) as the soundtrack for your video yearbook. These are guidelines, so you might be able to justify some addi- tional uses beyond them, but most uses of copyrighted works beyond these limitations require permission. These limitations are not undisputed and some sources argue that the primary factor for fair use is whether or not the new work is transformative, using the work for a very different purpose than the original. This approach allows for far more leeway for educational purposes (see Hobbs, 2010, and http://copyrightconfusion. wikispaces.com).

Finally, fair use applies only to works to which you have some legal right. This can be a problem for work that is posted on the web because much of what was posted was posted without permission (and is, thus, illegal). If the copyright owner has not given permis- sion for distribution, you do not have any right to the work. The primary offense is that of the person who illegally placed the work on the Internet, but you are liable as well if you also use the work. Unfortunately, it is not always easy to tell what work on the web is there legally. The web can be a great source of media, but much of it may consist of illegal postings.

Fair use gives you limited rights to use copyrighted material. As a teacher, you have the freedom to use some material in some ways that you (as an individual citizen) might not otherwise be allowed to use. Sometimes, delving through the complexity of fair use is worth the effort, so that you can use exactly what you need with a clear conscience even if it is copyrighted. However, for many things you want to do, there is a better way, as discussed in the following sections.

Copyleft, Creative Commons, and the Culture of Sharing

If the previous sections have scared you a bit, you are not alone. The strictness of copyright and the complexity of fair use appear to leave us with three unsatisfactory choices: Giving up and not using any media at all (my description of the culture of *no*); being very, very careful about what you use (the culture of *maybe*); or giving up and using whatever you want in whatever way you want without regard for the law (the culture of *yes*).

COPYLEFT

The term *copyleft* is often used to refer to mechanisms or licenses that allow the copyright holder to retain some rights while granting broad rights for others to use and share the material.

For more on copyleft, see *What is Copyleft?* (www.gnu.org/copyleft).

I have been teaching about copyright for many years, and I have never found any of these options satisfactory, but I have begrudgingly had to live with the culture of *maybe*, knowing that my students (and most teachers) are likely to pick the culture of *yes* or the culture of *no*.

Fortunately, a fourth option has emerged. It has been a theoretical option for many years because until recently, it wasn't a practical option for educators. Although Creative Commons licensing hasn't been applied to anywhere close to a majority of the media available, it has been applied to enough media to provide teachers with a rich stockpile of media to use for almost any purpose.

Search for a picture of a flower. An early 2012 search for hibiscus on http://images. google.com yielded over five million hits. If you need a picture of a hibiscus, there are more than enough here. But you are not allowed to use all of them beyond the fair use guidelines. How many do you need? If there were only one million available, would that be enough? What about 4,560? Perhaps 4,560 are enough, but that may be a small number if you have specific requirements or want a picture to illustrate an obscure topic. Google image search yielded 4,560 results for hibiscus pictures that are labeled for reuse. Fortunately, a similar search on Flickr yielded 26 thousand hibiscus pictures licensed with Creative Commons.

In the 5 million hibiscus pictures on Google, you are very likely to find exactly what you need. However, in the 26 thousand Creative Commons licensed pictures, you are only slightly less likely to find what you need. That is why Creative Commons has reached the tipping point. If a common search term only yielded a few dozen, or even a few hundred pictures, there would be a high probability of not finding what you want. Now that the search yields thousands, there is little need to rely on traditionally copyrighted material.

This is the culture of sharing. This new culture fits well with the broader cultural trends in which digital information flows freely, if not legally, around the Internet. The difference is that this culture of sharing is legal because it keeps the power to share in the hands of the content creators, and most are happy to share their own work. Now that enough content creators have chosen to share their work (this is true for digital images, as demonstrated above, and is quickly emerging for music and video as well), and tools such as Wikimedia Commons or Wiki-commons (http://en.wikipedia.org/wiki/ Wikimedia_Commons) and Flickr make it easy to do so, educational uses of media can make this cultural shift. Teachers can once again find sufficient media to use without worrying about ethical dilemmas. Further, teachers can now provide the honest and open culture of sharing as an alternative to students who are steeped in the illegal culture of *yes* (or mired in the restrictive culture of *no*).

The remainder of this chapter will outline the historical and philosophical background for the culture of sharing, give practical directions for finding and using media legally, and explain why, to be a full participant in the culture of sharing, you should share your creative works as well.

Philosophy and History

Lessig (2001, 2004) gives a complete history of the culture of sharing or what he calls "free culture." He quotes Richard Stallman, founder of the free software movement, in explaining that free culture is not like "free beer," but rather like "'free speech,' 'free markets,' 'free trade,' 'free enterprise,' 'free will,' and 'free elections'" (2004, p. xiv). Stallman advocates a world in which culture and cultural artifacts flow as freely as possible. This world is not without restrictions, constraints, controls, property rights, and profits, but it is a world in which those limitations on freedom are reasonable and kept from limiting free-flowing ideas and culture.

Lessig (2001) explains the concept of the commons as a resource that is free for public use. Sometimes a commons needs regulation and control to ensure its continued existence. This is true of physical resources, such as public parks (think of the Boston Common) and public roads. Being a commons doesn't mean that these resources can be used by anyone at any time without regard for others. But it does mean that:

> Anyone is free to access these spaces without first getting the permission of someone else. Access is not auctioned off to the highest bidder, and the right to control access is not handed off to some private or governmental entity. The resource … is made available to anyone. (Lessig, 2001, p. 20)

Lessig goes on to say, "Some are free in the sense that no price is paid. … Some are free even though a price may be paid (… as long as the fee is neutrally and consistently applied). … The essence, in other words, is that no one exercises the core of a property right with respect to these resources—the exclusive right to choose whether the resource is made available to others" (p. 20).

COPYRIGHT LAW

Copyright law does provide some protection for derivative works, particularly in the case of criticism, satire, and parody. Additionally, because of time limits, copyright law recognizes that eventually all work will join the commons. Lessig's ideas are an attempt to expand the commons.

Certain resources that might be part of the commons are rivalrous, while others are non-rivalrous. Rivalrous resources are limited and can be used up or otherwise overtaxed. If, for example, too many people enter a park at one time, they will not all fit. If, over time, too many people are careless with the park, its value to society might be diminished by overuse. If I have a book from the library, others cannot read that book until I return it.

Non-rivalrous resources are unlimited. These are not physical resources. Rather, they are such things as ideas and electronic expressions. For example, use of information on the Internet is non-rivalrous because one person's accessing it does not limit anyone else's ability to use it.

Lessig (2001) argues that Einstein's Theory of Relativity is an idea in the commons that is not diminished in any way by anyone's use of it (p. 20). Electronic resources, such as an electronic copy of this book, are non-rivalrous because distributing electronic copies, unlike physical copies, keeps the original intact. Of course, electronic copies of this book have copy protection that prevents unlimited sharing, making what was a non-rivalrous resource a rivalrous one. Although electronic distribution of creative works, such as this book as an e-book, might diminish the market value of the work, the distribution doesn't destroy the original. Lessig argues that overzealous control of creative works, by expansions of copyright law and corporate control, have diminished the value to society of the works. He would argue that my ability to write this chapter, by using and expanding on his ideas, is a small demonstration of the power of the commons.

The web, in general, is a great example of a commons, but both Lessig (2001) and Bollier (2003) argue that the commons is under attack with respect to information. Although the Internet started as a boon to information freedom, corporate and private interests are threatening the commons. Bollier says,

> The recurrent theme of enclosure is the conversion of commons into markets. Something that was available to all as a civic right is being privatized and commercialized. This not only pushes prices higher and forces people to obtain permission to use works that were previously free, it shifts ownership of resources from the American people to private companies. (p. 10)

Kiehl-Chisolm and Fitzgerald (2006) argue for a model of open access, giving everyone the right to access scientific and educational information. Lessig does not argue that there should be no property rights. Rather, he believes that those property rights need to be balanced with a flourishing commons. Lessig (2001, 2004) makes a strong philosophical case for his ideas, but if he stopped there, we would only be richer as students of philosophy and law. Fortunately, he has expanded his ideas to a practical application as one of the founders of Creative Commons. Creative Commons provides the tools and advocacy to make it possible to have flourishing commons in electronic media.

The Creative Commons

Creative Commons provides a mechanism for content creators to give permission in advance for others to use their work. Copyright applies the phrase "all rights reserved" to your work. Creative Commons applies the phrase "some rights reserved" (the Free Software Foundation advocates the phrase "all rights reversed").

The symbol for copyright is the letter *c* in a circle. The symbol for Creative Commons is the letters *cc* in a circle (Figure 7.1).

Figure 7.1 Creative Commons symbol, used under Creative Commons license (from http://creativecommons.org).

To find out if something is licensed under Creative Commons, look for the *cc* in a circle and/or the phrase "some rights reserved." If you see one or both of those things, you can generally click on them to get details about the type of license that has been assigned to the work. Go to http://creativecommons.org/about/licenses to see a variety of images you might see associated with a Creative Commons license. Figure 7.2 shows a sample Creative Commons License:

Figure 7.2 Examples of Creative Commons license image, used under Creative Commons license (from http://creativecommons.org).

This license has the *cc* in a circle followed by *BY* to indicate that users of this work must provide attribution (they must cite the source), and the *NC* to indicate that this can only be used without further permission for noncommercial purposes.

Do you create things to make money? I'm sure some of you do. I do. Although I had other reasons to write this book, making money from it was not at the bottom of the list. Do you create things without any intention of profiting? I'm sure all of you do. You write lesson plans. You take pictures on vacation of pretty scenery. You write explanations of concepts that are difficult for your students to understand. If colleagues asked you if they could use these things, most of the time you would be flattered and readily agree. You might already share some of this material freely on the web. The problem is that if others want to use your creations (in any ways beyond fair use), they are supposed to ask for permission. Remember, once you create something, it is automatically copyrighted. You might not mind a few quick emails asking for permission, but why be bothered? Creative Commons is a way for you to give permission in advance.

Even better, Creative Commons lets you retain the rights you want and give permission in advance for uses you don't mind. For example, you might not mind a teacher using your lesson plan in her classroom, but you might not want someone else to make money from it by publishing it in a book of lesson plans. In that case, you can give permission for noncommercial uses while not allowing commercial uses. Creative Commons allows you to choose the rights you want to retain by selecting the appropriate license. The terms can include the following conditions:

Attribution. All Creative Commons licenses require users to give attribution—that is, credit the source.

Commercial. You can decide whether users can use your work for commercial gain. This is not simply for selling your work but for using it in any commercial way. For example, a decorative picture on a monetized blog (one that has advertising to make money for the creator) is commercial. A picture used to make a point in a business presentation is commercial. A background photograph for your business card is commercial.

Modifications/Derivatives. You can decide whether to allow others to create derivative works from your works. That is, you can decide if they can modify or adapt your work or require them to distribute it as it is. This could include, for example, using an image editor to change a picture, rewriting the words to a song, using a song as synchronized background in a presentation, rewriting portions of a handout for their students to adapt it to their purposes, or creating a new work based on your original, such as a sequel to a book.

Share Alike. If you allow modifications, you can decide whether works based on your work must use a comparable license. Creative Commons is partly based on the GNU General Public License (GPL) from the Free Software Foundation, a licensing system that is mainly used for computer software. Share Alike (a Creative Commons attribution) is a cornerstone of GPL, forcing software developers who use resources from the community to put their derivative works back into the community. Making Share Alike an option instead of a requirement in Creative Commons is one source of tension between the Free Software Foundation and Creative Commons (Ciurcina, 2006).

For educators, you will find material that gives away some or all of those conditions, and you might choose to release material with some or all of those conditions.

Using the Commons

As a teacher using technology, you might want access to a number of things, such as pictures, music, videos, and text.

As you have learned from the fair use guidelines, if you want to use copyrighted pictures without permission, your rights are very limited. If you are creating a multimedia project, you can use a limited number of pictures from the same creator, you can load your project on a limited number of computers (far fewer than enough for your whole class), and you can use the project for a limited time. If I spend many hours creating something, I want to be able to use it with my students in whatever way I see fit for as long as it is still useful. The following are some tips for finding different types of media that are licensed with Creative Commons.

Pictures

Pictures with Creative Commons licensing are the easiest form of media to find. Here are some sources:

Advanced Flickr Search
www.flickr.com

> Go to Flickr and type your search term into the search box. After clicking the search button, you will see thumbnails of pictures for your search term. At the top of the screen next to another search box, you will see the words "Advanced Search." Click to get advanced search options. Scroll down to the bottom to see the Creative Commons section.
>
> You have three checkboxes:
>
> ☐ Check the first box, "Only search within Creative Commons–licensed content."
>
> ☐ If you are creating something that you are considering using in a commercial way, you should check the second box "Find content to use commercially," but this option will limit the number of results.
>
> ☐ For many of your purposes, you will also want to check the third box, "Find content to modify, adapt, or build upon." This gives you broad power to do what you want with the content, including changing it and building it into multimedia projects.

Hit the search button at the bottom, and you will see pictures that you are free to use. When you see the picture, look on the right side of the screen for the words "Some rights reserved." If you click on those words, you will see details of the Creative Commons license that has been applied to that picture. All licenses require attribution (you must give credit to the content creator). You will know whether commercial uses are allowed, based on the choices you selected in Advanced Search. You will also know whether or not you are allowed to modify, adapt, or build upon what you find, based on your choice in Advanced Search. Finally, you should be looking for whether you are required to "share alike." If the license specifies share alike, then anything you create with that content must be released with the same license. If you are not willing to share your work freely, then make sure that you don't select content that uses a share-alike license.

Google Image Search

http://images.google.com

Go to Google Images and click on "Advanced Image Search." Under usage rights, you can choose not filtered by license, labeled for reuse, labeled for commercial reuse, labeled for reuse with modification, or labeled for commercial reuse with modification. For educational purposes, your safest choice is labeled for reuse with modification. This will find some pictures from Flickr and from other sources. When you find pictures in this way, be sure to go to the original source to find out the details of the licensing. Often you will readily find the specific Creative Commons license associated with a picture, a notice that the picture is in the public domain, or a notice that the picture is licensed with the GNU Free Documentation license (see www.gnu. org/licenses/gfdl.html). Other times you might not find a license; when this happens, it is best not to use the work.

Wikimedia Commons

http://commons.wikimedia.org

Go to the website and search. When you click on the thumbnail of a picture, you can scroll below the picture to find the details of licensing associated with it.

Other sources

There are other sources of pictures that have given permission without ascribing a specific license. Many of them allow educational use of their pictures. See, for example, http://pics4learning.com and http://classroomclipart.com. Adam and Mowers (2008) provide other options for searching for copyright-friendly content.

Music and Sounds

Although pictures are the easiest media to find in copyright-friendly format, the web contains a great deal of music and sounds. Here are some sources:

Opsound

http://opsound.org

Many songs and albums, organized by genre

ccMixter

http://ccmixter.org

Many songs and albums, organized by artist

Jamendo

www.jamendo.com

Many songs and albums

ArtistServer

www.artistserver.com

Many songs and albums; check for specific licensing

Free-Loops.com

http://free-loops.com

Loops and sound effects; watch for different licensing for different sounds

Freesound
www.freesound.org

User-uploaded sounds; watch out for inappropriate content

Videos

Videos licensed with Creative Commons are harder to find than other types of media. TeacherTube (http://teachertube.com) contains language in its license agreement that all videos uploaded are licensed under Creative Commons; this wording is buried in the license agreement, so those who upload videos might not be aware that they are assigning a Creative Commons license, and of greater concern, they might not be the owners of the material they upload. Before using video from TeacherTube, you should check to see that the person who uploaded it is the creator of the video. You might also find a limited selection of videos at the following sites:

http://wiki.creativecommons.org/Video
http://en.wikipedia.org/wiki/List_of_open_content_films

Always be sure to check the licensing for any video that you find. Note that if you want to show pieces of video for educational (not entertainment) purposes in your classroom, you have some rights to do that under fair use if you show the minimum necessary for your educational purpose.

You will need copyright-friendly licensing if you are planning to incorporate the video into your own work.

Text and Other Sources

Many general search engines allow you to search for content by the type of license. Some include media only, while others include text as well. Here are some good starting points:

CC Search
http://search.creativecommons.org

Search a variety of Creative Commons content; always double-check license.

Google

www.google.com

> Perform a regular search and look for the Options button at the top right of the screen (it looks like a gear) and choose "Advanced Search." Scroll down to the bottom of the screen and choose from the drop-down usage rights menu.

SpinXpress

http://spinxpress.com/getmedia

> Search by media type and license type.

Wikimedia Commons

http://commons.wikimedia.org

> Browse by category.

Participate in the Culture of Sharing

Creative Commons works, in a practical sense, because thousands of people have chosen to share millions of creative works with others. Becoming part of that community of sharing strengthens the community. Kranich (2003) says, "Without a sophisticated information commons in every community, we cannot ensure the public's right to know" (p. 24). That is, you should consider licensing your own work with a Creative Commons license. See Johnstone (2003) for an overview of the process of sharing material while retaining your own rights to it, or simply go to http://creativecommons.org/choose/ and select a license to place on your work.

The rise of Creative Commons has been great for educators, but other trends are causing problems. The commercialization of the Internet has been an issue for free material, but now the trend is to monetize everything. Someone who might write a blog to share educational tips is now likely to try to set that up as a source of revenue by selling advertising on the blog (this takes only a few minutes with tools such as Google AdSense). I don't begrudge anyone the right to make money, but for most creators of educational blogs or sites, the potential profit is close to zero, while the potential good to make the work freely available is large. The cultural trend of monetization closes creators off to sharing freely.

Another trend that is problematic is the trend to lock information behind passwords. Most colleges and universities (as well as many K–12 schools) have course management systems available, such as Blackboard and Moodle. These are great tools for organizing online material. The problem is that, by default, the material you share is only open to students registered for the course. Some schools, such as MIT (through the Massachusetts Institute of Technology OpenCourseWare project—see http://ocw.mit.edu) are taking intentional steps to make as much material as possible open (and with the new edX collaboration with Harvard University, they are looking to make entire courses available for free online). Most schools, however, and the teachers and professors who teach there, use the tools provided to them without concern for the culture of sharing.

This is why it is important to be conscious of the culture of sharing and make free as much of your own material as possible. This starts with simply making the material available to others and not locking it behind firewalls and passwords. Additionally, using sites, like Flickr, that have built-in mechanisms for assigning Creative Commons licenses gives others access and the right to use your material. Alternatively, you can add a Creative Commons license to any material you put on the web by getting the license material from http://creativecommons.org.

In Flickr, you can either adjust the permission for an individual photo (or group of photos), or you can set your default to include a Creative Commons license. When you see an individual picture, you can look for the copyright notice under "Additional Information" on the right side of the screen. Click "Edit." Then choose the specific license you want, based on the restrictions you want to place on the photo (deciding whether you want to allow commercial uses, allow modifications/derivative works, and whether others are required to share alike). That's it.

However, you can make it easier for yourself by setting up your personal preferences to default to a Creative Commons license. If there is any picture that you don't want to share (or want it to have a different license), you can always use the above procedure to assign copyright. To change your default setting (so that all new uploads will have Creative Commons licensing unless you specify otherwise), go to your account and click on the "Privacy and Permission" tab. Scroll down to the "Defaults for New Uploads" section and click "Edit" next to "What license will your content have." From there, you can add one of the Creative Commons licenses as your default setting. This won't change any photos you have already uploaded, but it will impact any new photos you upload.

If you don't use a system that has Creative Commons built in, then you can visit the Creative Commons website, and click on the link for "License." Decide the type of license you want, and add the additional information about where to find the content and how to contact you about additional licensing. You will be taken to a page that gives you a choice of icons to use and some HTML code to embed on your site. Don't worry if you are not an HTML guru. Most web systems (such as blogs) have a simple way to view the HTML or add HTML. All you have to do is paste the HTML code into an editor that understands HTML, and the license will appear on your site. Further instructions can be found at the publishing tutorial on the Creative Commons website, http://wiki.creativecommons.org/Website/Publish.

The only caveat is that a Creative Commons license is not revocable. That is, once you release something with Creative Commons, you can't take it back. You are under no obligation to continue to distribute it with a Creative Commons license, and you are free to distribute additional copies with an "all rights reserved" copyright associated with it, but the copies that are already floating around will retain the Creative Commons license. For most of your purposes, this will have little impact. You might choose to create handouts for a class and release them under Creative Commons. As the handouts grow, you might find that you want to publish the handouts as a book with all rights reserved. Yes, your Creative Commons handouts might still be floating around, but you can take down your own website and point browsers to your book.

We all create content. For the most part, we would be thrilled if someone thought our work were good enough to use and would happily give it away as long as we get credit for creating it. Creative Commons formalizes and simplifies this process, so we can make our content available to others easily. It is easy to do and benefits the community of learners.

Creative Commons and Student-Created Work

While we take it for granted that teachers create content, let's remember that students also create content. Most students enjoy sharing their work, especially when teachers tell them it's worth sharing—not only with others in the classroom but with students around the world who can access their creations online.

When dealing with student-created work, teachers need to be very careful to inform parents and get parental consent if the teacher is going to be the one sharing the work online or even with other students. When students hand in work to teachers, teachers do not own it—they are not the copyright holders. Many school districts have blanket forms that parents sign at the beginning of the school year to allow (or to opt out of) sharing student work in a variety of ways. While this might seem like a silly formality, remember that Creative Commons is not about usurping the rights of copyright holders but about giving copyright holders the ability to expand the allowed use of their works. Also, remember that Creative Commons does not override plagiarism. All Creative Commons-licensed work requires attribution. With or without Creative Commons, more and more resources are available to students online, and teachers need to be smart about creating assignments that challenge students to build upon, analyze, and connect ideas and not merely regurgitate them.

Conclusion

As copyright and controls become stricter, the need for mechanisms to keep some content free becomes greater. Creative Commons is one such mechanism, and it is one that has reached a tipping point, making a variety of content widely available for educational use. Educators still need a working knowledge of copyright laws, including fair use and its limitations, but using traditionally copyrighted material is no longer the first option. Furthermore, to keep the momentum going, educators should be licensing their own material with culture of sharing mechanisms, such as Creative Commons. The culture of sharing described in this chapter is an important antidote to the restrictions of copyright and the ethical dilemma faced by educators who want to follow legal and ethical standards while using material that others have created.

Exercises

1. Create a one-page guide to copyright law for your students.

2. Create a one-page guide to copyright law for other teachers.

3. Pick a topic and find 10 pictures with Creative Commons licensing that help to explain that topic. Use a tool like Microsoft's Photo Story 3 or Apple's iMovie to create a short video about the topic, using the pictures you found, narration that you record, and background sound that you find with Creative Commons licensing. As an alternative, create a digital story (see, for example, the Center for Digital Storytelling at www.storycenter.org

and the Digital Storytelling Classroom Project at www.epals.com/projects/info.aspx?DivID=Digital_overview) using Creative Commons–licensed media.

4. Create your own copyright law. Decide what you think would be fair for others to use of the works you create and for you to use of what others create. For this exercise, only think about what you think would be fair, not what the law actually says. As an alternative, work in a group and take different roles (such as author, teacher, student, music publisher, struggling musician, librarian, and others) and ask the role-players to discuss what they think would be fair from their own perspectives.

References

Adam, A., & Mowers, H. (2008). Start your search engines, part two. *School Library Journal, 54*(5), 58–60.

Bollier, D. (2003). Saving the information commons. *Knowledge Quest, 31*(4), 9–12.

Ciurcina, M. (2006, March 14). Free software, free knowledge. Retrieved December 11, 2009, from http://www.creativecommons.it/ciurcina

CONFU: The Conference on Fair Use. (1996). *Fair use guidelines for educational multimedia* [Interim report]. Washington, DC: U.S. Patent and Trademark Office. http://copyright.lib.utexas.edu/ccmcguid.html

Davidson, H. (2002, October 15). The educator's guide to copyright and fair use. *Technology & Learning, 23*(3). Retrieved from http://www.techlearning.com/db_area/archives/TL/2002/10/copyright.html

Free Software Foundation. (2009). What is copyleft? Retrieved December 11, 2009, from http://www.gnu.org/copyleft

Harper, G. K., & University of Texas at Austin. (2001, 2007). Copyright crash course. Retrieved December 11, 2009, from http://copyright.lib.utexas.edu/confu.html

Hobbs, R. (2010). *Copyright clarity: How fair use supports digital learning.* Thousand Oaks, CA: Corwin.

Johnson, D. (2009). Creative Commons and why it should be more commonly understood. *Library Media Connection, 27*(6), 56–57.

Johnstone, S. M. (2003). Sharing educational materials without losing rights. *Change: The Magazine of Higher Learning, 35*(6), 49–51.

Kiel-Chisholm, S., & Fitzgerald, B. (2006). The rise of open access in the Creative, Educational and Science Commons. *Policy Futures in Education 4*(4), 366–379.

Kranich, N. (2003). Staking a claim in the information commons. *Knowledge Quest 31*(4), 22–25.

Lehman, B. A. (1998). *The Conference on Fair Use: Final report to the commissioner on the conclusion of the Conference on Fair Use.* Washington, DC: U.S. Patent and Trademark Office. Retrieved from http://www.uspto.gov/web/offices/dcom/olia/confu/confurep.pdf

Lessig, L. (2001). *The future of ideas: The fate of the commons in a connected world.* New York, NY: Random House.

Lessig, L. (2004). *Free culture: How big media uses technology and the law to lock down culture and control creativity.* New York, NY: The Penguin Press.

Marcovitz, D. M. (2006). Copyright, technology, and your rights. In R. C. Hunter (Series Ed.) & S. Y. Tettegah (Vol. Ed.), *Advances in educational administration*: Vol. 8. *Technology and education: Issues in administration, policy, and applications in K12 schools* (pp. 73–84). London, UK: Elsevier.

Marcovitz, D. M. (2012). *Powerful PowerPoint for educators: Using Visual Basic for Applications to make PowerPoint interactive* (2nd ed.). Westport, CT: Libraries Unlimited.

Salpeter, J. (2008, October 15). The new rules of copyright. *Tech & Learning, 6*, 33–36. Available at http://www.techlearning.com/article/the-new-rules-of-copyright/45424

University of St. Francis. (2004). A visit to copyright bay. http://web.archive.org/web/20080705231404/http://www.stfrancis.edu/cid/copyrightbay/mmcr1.htm

U.S. Copyright Office. (2009). Copyright Law of the United States and Related Laws Contained in Title 17 of the United States Code. Retrieved December 11, 2009, from http://www.copyright.gov/title17 (For the text of title 17, including all amendments enacted through December 9, 2010, see www.copyright.gov/title17/circ92.pdf).

CHAPTER EIGHT

Digital Citizenship in a Dangerous World

In *Watch IT,* Burbules and Callister (2000) warn:

> The blanket approach of trying to weed out the bad while retaining the good cannot take into account the complexity of learning and knowledge, and the diversity and diverse needs of learners.
>
> This, then, is the educational challenge: helping students learn to operate in an environment that is inherently "dangerous," to deal with what may be unexpected or unpleasant, to make critical judgments about what they find. (p. 118)

The web is a dangerous place. There are scammers, hackers, pornographers, sexual predators, and a variety of people doing all kinds of mean, nasty stuff. Because of this, many schools implement strict policies and procedures and technical fixes in an attempt to prevent anything bad happening. As a parent, I am scared. One of the worst things I can imagine is one of my daughters being assaulted by a sexual predator she met online. It's easy to be scared, but it's much harder to act rationally and thoughtfully. The reality is that much of what we do to keep our students safe online is counterproductive; instead, our fearful, overprotective measures prevent them from learning the skills to keep themselves safe.

Matt Levinson in *From Fear to Facebook* (2010) says:

> Schools have to take precautionary, protective measures to keep online usage at school safe, but given the nature of the global marketplace, it is unrealistic to think that schools can keep everything out. Instead, schools should capitalize on teachable moments that arise when students encounter hateful language on a blog post or false claims on a website. Examine the intent, explore the bias, strategize a response, and invite the students to develop a solution. Every parent and educator wants students to make sensible decisions when they are on their own out in the world. Students are deprived of precious learning opportunities under the guidance and care of adults who care about them if schools and parents block their online access. (pp. 69–70)

What Are the Dangers?

Burbules and Callister (2000) discuss "The 4 M's": misinformation, malinformation, messed-up information, and mostly useless information.

Misinformation is information that is wrong or incomplete in intentional or unintentional ways. It might be someone's attempt to deceive, it might be an honest mistake, or it might be one viewpoint among many.

Malinformation is the information we generally try to block, such as pornography, hate group propaganda, and dangerous material.

Messed-up information is not necessarily bad or wrong but so poorly organized that it is barely usable.

Mostly useless information includes the trivia and nonsense that permeate the web (see, for example, Lolcats at http://icanhascheezburger.com).

In addition to the 4 M's, we need to be concerned about inappropriate interactions. These can include interactions with sexual predators and cyberbullies. Additionally, although this falls under mostly useless information, we have to be concerned with the seductive nature of the web for games and social interaction. We can't allow our students to be distracted all day from the important task of learning.

Picture the following classroom. The classroom is awash with technology. Students are playing games while the teacher is talking. Other students are posting nasty messages about their teachers and other students on Facebook. Some students are texting test answers to their friends. Before class, students are giggling in the back while looking at some inappropriate pictures online. The teacher seems to be in control, but the students are paying little attention to what is happening in the classroom.

Picture another classroom. This classroom also has an abundance of technology. Students are communicating with other classrooms via ePals to discuss the novel they just read. Other students are uploading data from the class weather station to a database that is shared with other classes. Some students are exploring a wide range of viewpoints on climate change, and the teacher is chatting with them about some wild claims they just found. Other students are commenting on the teacher's podcast at VoiceThread. A reading group is preparing questions for the book author who will be joining them for a brief discussion on Skype.

These two classrooms represent the opposite ends of the spectrum. We are afraid of the first classroom. We are so afraid that we will do whatever we can to stop it. But what if that prevents us from having the second classroom? The reality is that the only way to stop all misuse of technology is to ban all technology—and then search all students as they enter the school to make sure they aren't sneaking in a smartphone to get around the bans. Short of that, we do our best to filter out anything that might have questionable content.

> The practice of filtering, of blocking targeted information, tears holes in the fabric of knowledge and understanding.
>
> Knowledge, creativity, critical thinking, discernment, wisdom—these are not about the accumulation of facts. They are about the relations between ideas, information, ethics, and culture. (Burbules & Callister, 2000, p. 108)

That leads us to the second classroom. We want that, but to get there, we need to have a great deal of freedom. We might choose to allow anything and leave the filters wide open. But what if that devolves into the first classroom?

What we need is a balanced solution. No solution will be perfect, but too many schools have leaned too far toward preventing the first scenario, which has the side effect of preventing the second. So what can you do?

You need filters. Very few schools choose to do without filters entirely. If you have influence over your school's policies, do what you can to create a quick and easy process for overriding the filters. For safety reasons, someone on site should have the ability to override the filters, and that person should be able to grant any teacher temporary access to anything he or she needs for educational purposes. Permanently unblocking a site might require a more detailed review, but a temporary override should be quick and easy. If you don't have influence over your school's policies, become familiar with the system in place for overriding filters. Plan in advance and apply for overrides to the filter as far in advance as possible. Do this even for sites that are not currently blocked because you never know when the system will decide to block something you need.

Monitor your students. With or without filters, students can get to inappropriate material. Appropriate supervision is always required.

Teach your students what to do when they come across inappropriate material. This might involve simply hitting the back button on the browser, turning off the monitor, closing the laptop, and raising their hands to await the teacher. It is easy to come across inappropriate material accidentally through a search or mistyped address—www.whitehouse.com used to be a pornography site accidentally reached by unsuspecting people who were interested in seeing what the president was up to.

Educate your students about what is expected of them and how technology can benefit them. Create an acceptable use policy (AUP) or responsible use policy for your classroom or your school. Many school systems have detailed and legalistic AUPs. The lawyers might require it, but your students can't understand it. Write something they can understand that lays out a positive perspective for them and their parents. Or, better yet, have them help you write it. Some of the best acceptable use policies I have seen are based on positive behavior systems that are already part of the school culture.

Get the parents on your side. If they expect that their children will never see anything that is remotely inappropriate, you will have to lock everything down. If you can explain to them how you will use the messy web to help their children become 21st-century learners, including teaching them how to deal with something inappropriate when it sneaks through, you can get the parents to support what you want to do and not go running to the principal the first time something goes wrong.

Use mishaps as teachable moments. If you create a caring culture of innovation, your students will teach you as you guide them.

The Biggest Risks

Nancy Willard (n.d.) is concerned that we are focused on the wrong risks to online activity:

> Over the last decade, much of the Internet safety material … contains disinformation which creates the fear that young people are at high risk of online sexual predation, when the actual research and arrest data indicates the opposite. There is a tendency among law enforcement officials to think that scare tactics are effective in reducing risk behavior. Research has never found this to be so.

When the scare tactics turn out to be overstated, kids catch on quickly and stop listening. Meanwhile, in our attempts to build higher and higher fences, we end up depriving students of opportunities to learn important information and interaction skills. Additionally, in our reliance on technical means of protecting children, we seek technological fixes to repair what are in reality social problems.

In 1966, Alvin Weinberg coined the phrase *technological fix*. He was concerned that social problems are complex, and when we try to fix them with technology, the solution is partial, tenuous, and fraught with unintended consequences. He was discussing the proliferation of nuclear weapons as a deterrent to war. In his example, one of his concerns was that the presence of nuclear weapons would diminish the use and benefits of diplomacy. Although I hesitate to take an analogy too far between war and dangers on the Internet or nuclear weapons and filters, the consequences of each technological fix diminish the important and subtle interactions between people (national leaders on the one hand and teachers and students on the other).

We need to recognize that most of the students who are at risk online are also at risk offline. The report of the Internet Safety Technical Taskforce (2008, p. 4) states:

> Minors are not equally at risk online. Those who are most at risk often engage in risky behaviors and have difficulties in other parts of their lives. The psychosocial makeup of and family dynamics surrounding particular minors are better predictors of risk than the use of specific media or technologies.

Willard (2010) expands on this:

> Young people who are in the greatest risk online are the ones who are already at greater risk in the Real World. These risks include risky sexual activities, cyberbullying, unsafe or dangerous online communities, addictive access, posting unsafe or hurtful material, communicating in unsafe environments, and engaging in harmful communications. These "at risk" young people are likely to also
>
> - Have significant psychosocial concerns—including depression, social anxiety, anger responses, and suicidal ideation.
>
> - Engage in other "real world" risk taking behavior—drug abuse, alcohol, and self-harm.
>
> - Be victims of physical and sexual abuse—and engage in physical and sexual aggression.
>
> - Have friends who are also "at risk."
>
> - Have poor relations with parents or other caregivers. (pp. 11–12)

In *Katie.com: My Story* (2000), Katherine Tarbox describes her encounter as a young teenager with a sexual predator after meeting him online. You would expect the book to lead you to fear the dangers of the Internet, but my conclusion and the conclusion of most of my students who read it was that it was the story of a troubled girl. The Internet just happened to be one part of her trouble.

This is not to say that we should have no concern about sexual predators, but exaggerating this possibility as the primary risk of using the Internet is shortsighted and misrepresents reality. When we tell our students they can't communicate online because there is a sexual predator lurking on every website, we not only block them from valuable educational opportunities, we also lose their trust by telling them something that is of limited truth and totally counter to their experience. In reality, most children are at much greater risk of inappropriate interactions with their peers, including cyberbullying.

Cyberbullying

What is cyberbullying?

> Cyberbullying is bullying or harassment that happens online.
> It can happen in an email, a text message, an online game, or
> comments on a social networking site. It might involve rumors or
> images posted on someone's profile or passed around for others
> to see, or creating a group or page to make a person feel left out.
> (Federal Trade Commission, 2010, p. 21; http://onguardonline.gov/
> articles/0028-cyberbullying)

I remember my childhood as a cruel time. Kids will be kids, and kids can be mean. Kids can tease and even bully. As much of children's lives has moved online, the meanness has moved online as well. And just as positive messages can be multiplied online, so, too, can negative messages. I remember in middle school when Deana told me that she would "tell everyone and I would be ruined" (I don't think I even knew at the time what she was going to tell everyone about me). The ruin never came. I'm sure she told her friends, who may or may not have told their friends, and I was the source of some ridicule behind my back, but word never got back to me, and it had little or no impact on my life. Imagine the same scenario today, except that the dreadful insult or insinuation were posted on my Facebook wall or circulated in an online burn book. The kinds of comments that might reach a few people and soon be forgotten can be magnified by the Internet to reach thousands of people and remain online permanently.

Unlike attacks by sexual predators, cyberbullying is likely to affect your school. In an article about a recent survey, Khadaroo (2010) states, "More than half of American teens … know someone their age who has been targeted by hurtful electronic communications. Nearly a third have been targets themselves." Numbers like this are scary, but they are overhyped. Being "targeted by hurtful electronic communication" is not the same as cyberbullying, and more than half knowing someone who has been targeted doesn't mean that half have been targeted (a handful of students in a school could be targeted, and more than half the school might know about it). Similar surveys have been used to overhype the sexual nature of the Internet. Large percentages of teens have received messages with unwanted sexual content, but the hype distorts that into the "fact" that the same percentage of teens have been the target of sexual predators. Although I believe that cyberbullying is a real danger among teens and can have severe consequences for emotional and physical well-being, it is not helpful to exaggerate the scope of the problem.

When my daughter was in eighth grade, she was involved in a dispute among a group of students. The dispute led to an angry exchange on the Facebook wall of the students. I was terrified for her. Although my daughter wasn't involved in the Facebook exchange (other than reading it on the wall), I could easily see this escalating. Fortunately, the exchange on Facebook was no more than the equivalent of a yelling match in the cafeteria (except that a few hundred more people saw the Facebook posts than would have seen an in-person yelling match), and it didn't escalate, but teens feel empowered (everyone, really, but teens particularly) in good and bad ways online. This has been true since the beginning of the Internet. "Flame wars" have erupted in listservs and news-groups and chat rooms. The difference is that now these battles are personal and coming from people you know and care about. One angry Facebook wall post can turn into a heated exchange that travels around the school and the Internet as tensions rise, leading to significant, real hurts in a real social circle, both online and offline.

Willard (2007a) categorizes cyberbullying as taking the following forms:

- **flaming** "a heated, short-lived argument that occurs between two or more protagonists" (p. 5)

- **harassment** "repeated, ongoing sending of offensive messages to an individual target" (p. 6)

- **denigration** "speech about a target that is harmful, untrue, or cruel" (p. 7)

- **impersonation** "the cyberbully gains the ability to impersonate the target and post material that reflects badly on the target or interferes with the target's friendships" (p. 8)

- **outing and trickery** "publicly posting, sending, or forwarding personal communica-tions or images, especially communications or images that contain intimate personal information or are potentially embarrassing" (p. 9)

- **exclusion** "the designation of who is a member of the in-group and who is an outcast" (p. 9)

- **cyberstalking** "repeated sending of harmful messages that include threat of harm are highly intimidating or extremely offensive" (p. 10)

- **cyberthreats** "statements of intent to hurt someone or commit suicide" or "material that provides clues that the person ... may be considering hurting someone, self-harm, or suicide" (p. 11)

Although any of these can be disturbing, they reach the level of cyberbullying when they are repeated over time. A single denigrating wall posting, for example, is not cyberbullying. (For more information, go to www.embracingdigitalyouth.org/reports-issue-briefs/issue-briefs/educators-guide/.)

Most U.S. schools receive funding for Internet access via the Federal Communication Commission's (FCC) E-Rate Program. That funding already requires schools to have instruction about online safety and use some kind of filtering to protect children. The FCC (2011) reports:

> Beginning July 1, 2012, schools' Internet safety policies must provide for educating minors about appropriate online behavior, including interacting with other individuals on social networking websites and in chat rooms and cyberbullying awareness and response. (http://hraunfoss.fcc.gov/edocs_public/attachmatch/FCC-11-125A1.pdf)

Educating students about cyberbullying is an important step, but discipline over incidents of cyberbullying can be tricky. If the cyberbullying takes place outside of school, schools have limited rights to discipline students for it. The standard that limits a school's ability to act is from the 1969 Supreme Court decision "Tinker v. The Des Moines Independent Community School District" (see www.law.cornell.edu/supct/html/historics/USSC_CR_0393_0503_ZS.html), in which it states that students have a right to free speech, and the schools can only discipline students if the speech could cause a "material and substantial disruption" to the educational process. The Tinker decision has been used in cases of cyberbullying, including a recent case in California in which a school was successfully sued after suspending an eighth grade girl for posting a video on YouTube in which she and her friends called another student a "slut" and other mean things.

The 1969 Tinker case was about the students' right to wear black armbands to protest the Vietnam War. This is a far cry from cyberbullying. When teachers and principals try to prevent or quell cyberbullying, they are put in a very difficult situation. Clearly, an online discussion of a plan to start a fight at school could be used to discipline students, but what about cyberbullying that could lead to physical harm in school and might make victims afraid to come to school? This is a gray area that the law does not clearly address. Schools need to be very concerned about the safety of their students, but they must balance that with the free speech rights of their students.

Discipline and action are not the same thing. It is true that a school might be sued for disciplining a student for exercising free speech rights, but nonpunitive counseling and education can be appropriate. Just like responses to bullying in general, schools need to maintain open lines of communication with students (the bully and the bullied) and parents. Students should know that there are trusted adults to whom they can talk when there is a problem. Schools also need to be sure that the filter doesn't get in the way of an effective response to bullying. Does your school block Facebook? What if the bullying took place on Facebook? Someone in your school should be able to override any filter to investigate.

Willard (2007a) suggests a multipronged approach to cyberbullying that includes coordinated planning with the school's safety committee; needs assessment of staff and students; a review of policies at the school and/or district level; an effective reporting, review, and response process; parent outreach; community outreach; student education; and performance measurement and evaluation. For more details about this process, see Willard (2007a, 2007b). Because taking action against cyberbullying is an important part of school safety, it is important that technology experts and technology committees come together with safety and counseling experts and committees. Cyberbullying cannot merely be the responsibility of the technology people in the school, and if members of the safe schools committee are not knowledgeable about technology, it cannot be their responsibility alone.

A needs assessment among students can help to determine the extent of the problem and raise awareness. A staff needs assessment—or a discussion among key technology, counseling, and safe schools staff—can help to understand the current state of policies and procedures for dealing with cyberbullying. Needs assessments can also serve as baseline data for comparative purposes while evaluating progress.

All school staff need to be made aware of issues around cyberbullying. Willard (2007b) recommends a triage approach, in which several key people need a high level of expertise about cyberbullying. First responders (including administrators, counselors, and computer teachers) need an understanding of how to detect problems and intervene when necessary. Teachers who teach students about cyberbullying will need effective ways to raise awareness and motivate safe and responsible behavior.

Parents and community members need to be made aware of issues with cyberbullying and learn how they can detect problems and intervene when necessary. They also need strategies to empower their children not to accept bullying tacitly by being passive bystanders.

Student education is a key part of the process. This doesn't have to be in the form of separate cyberbullying lessons but can be part of a larger curriculum about being safe and responsible digital citizens. Students should know that there are consequences to being mean online, and they should be aware that children can be bullies, victims, or bystanders. They should know about confidential school processes for seeking out trusted adults in any role that they might play in responding to victims and taking actions against the perpetrators of cyberbullying. As Willard (2007b) says, "Educating bystanders about the importance of speaking out, providing assistance to victims and reporting concerns is important" (p. 13).

Children's Internet Protection Act

The Children's Internet Protection Act (CIPA) is a law that requires most schools and libraries to take certain Internet safety measures. The Federal Communication Commission's fact sheet about CIPA (FCC, 2009) states the following under the heading, What CIPA Requires:

■ Schools and libraries subject to CIPA may not receive the discounts offered by the E-Rate program unless they certify that they have an Internet safety policy that includes technology protection measures. The protection measures must block or filter Internet access to pictures that are: (a) obscene, (b) child pornography, or (c) harmful to minors (for computers that are accessed by minors). Before adopting this Internet safety policy, schools and libraries must provide reasonable notice and hold at least one public hearing or meeting to address the proposal.

■ Schools subject to CIPA are required to adopt and enforce a policy to monitor online activities of minors.

■ Schools and libraries subject to CIPA are required to adopt and implement an Internet safety policy addressing: (a) access by minors to inappropriate matter on the Internet; (b) the safety and security of minors when using electronic mail, chat rooms, and other forms of direct electronic communications; (c) unauthorized access, including so-called "hacking," and other unlawful activities by minors online; (d) unauthorized disclosure, use, and dissemination of personal information regarding minors; and (e) measures restricting minors' access to materials harmful to them.

If you know anything at all about CIPA, you know that it requires your school to have an acceptable use policy (AUP) and to block anything that might be inappropriate. The problem is that CIPA doesn't say that. First, CIPA only applies to schools that accept

E-Rate funding. Because almost all schools in the United States accept E-Rate funding, it probably applies to your school. Second, it does require a plan and filtering, but it doesn't specify that the filtering has to block anything that might be inappropriate. It simply requires blocking images that are obscene, child pornography, or harmful to minors and only for computers accessed by minors. Your school or district almost certainly has filtering in place that goes far beyond what the law requires, so don't use (or let your administration use) CIPA as an excuse to block more than is necessary. Instead, you should think, as a school or district, about what is and is not appropriate. You might find that you want to block minimally and put in place educational programs and policies that cover inappropriate use.

Additionally, any policy that you implement should allow for adults to override the filter as allowed by the law: "An authorized person may disable the blocking or filtering measure during use by an adult to enable access for bona fide research or other lawful purposes" (FCC, 2009; see www.fcc.gov/guides/childrens-internet-protection-act).

Although the law's requirements are minimal, they provide a good framework for action: minimal filtering and policies and procedures to monitor use and teach safe and responsible Internet use.

Nancy Willard (2003, Part II, Chapter 1, pp. 3–4) asks the following questions:

WILLARD'S QUESTIONS REMAIN RELEVANT

Not enough has changed in the past decade. I had the opportunity to discuss these district preparedness questions with Nancy Willard in 2012. She wrote them back in 2003 (an eternity ago in terms of technology), and we both agreed that it is unfortunate that these questions are still relevant today as so little has progressed on this front.

■ Does your district have full and complete knowledge of what sites are being blocked and the basis upon which these decisions are made? Have the companies made full public disclosure of this information as necessary to ensure public accountability?

■ Has the determination of which categories of material should be blocked been made by school administrators, in accord with the district's determination of what kinds of material should be considered to be inappropriate, and with full knowledge of the kinds of material blocked in those categories? Or has the district's technology services personnel or the filtering company made the determination of what categories are blocked (district using company's default setting)?

- Has the district set the filter to block many categories, which significantly increases the rate of overblocking, or has the district set the filter to block only the categories necessary to be blocked under CIPA?

- Has the district established effective procedures to override the filter in cases when the filter is blocking access to educational material or any material students have a constitutional right to access? Does this process ensure rapid response? Have procedures been established to allow students to anonymously request a site be overridden to allow for access to sensitive material?

CIPA places some requirements on you, but as long as you are blocking obscene images and thinking about educating students to be responsible digital citizens, you are likely to be covering CIPA's requirements. That leaves you to create or use smart policies and curricula that promote responsible use, while allowing for your students to consume, create, and interact online in appropriate ways.

Filters

It has been said that filters are like suntan lotion—allowing you to stay out in the sun a little longer, but you can still get burned (NPR, 1997). Additionally, any school receiving certain federal funding, such as E-Rate funding, is required to use filtering to block obscene pictures. The problem isn't filters themselves but relying on filters as a complete plug-and-play solution.

One of the dangers of filters is complacency. Teachers who think filters are perfect are less likely to monitor their students' online activity. It can be even worse for parents who let their children lock themselves in their rooms for hours on the Internet unsupervised. Further, administrators who think that filters are perfect will find they are locking out some of the best material on the web. I am not suggesting that schools shouldn't use filters; I am suggesting that we not rely on them as the only solution and that we have policies that make it easy for teachers to override the filters (or have them overridden) when there is an appropriate educational need.

Filters are increasingly being used not only to block specific content but also to block Web 2.0 tools. These tools are generally open so that anyone can post anything, and they do, which is why they are blocked. But blocking them eliminates useful tools. Administrators who rely on the filters too much will be happy about all the inappropriate content that is blocked without thinking about the consequences. On the one hand, they want teachers to use technology; on the other hand, they put up roadblocks. Every roadblock makes it more likely that teachers will give up. And what they're giving up are powerful learning experiences that can help students learn content and become 21st-century learners. Just this week, some of my students, who are also K–12 teachers, reported that a tool we have been using in class was blocked by their school system's filter without notice. As teachers, they can apply to have it unblocked, but the process can take months. In the meantime, any plans they have to use this tool have to be put on hold. What's worse is that they are no longer excited about using any web tools in their classrooms because their plans can be blocked at any time. When it takes months to unblock a useful site, the safety process has become far too cumbersome, preventing rather than incentivizing innovation in schools.

Teachers should work with the school or district process to understand what is and is not blocked and how they can get appropriate sites and tools unblocked. If the process is cumbersome, they should work to change the process. This can happen by creating valuable lessons that rely on material or tools that might be blocked. If you can demonstrate why the blocked material is valuable and how you will monitor use to keep students safe, you'll be more likely to convince your administration to grant you access.

Teaching Digital Citizenship

Terms like acceptable use policy (AUP) and Internet safety are bandied about, usually as isolated entities. That is, we write an AUP, make people read it on the first day of school, and forget about it. We give a brief lesson on avoiding bad people or bad sites online and forget about it. Instead, as David Warlick (2008) suggests, we need an AUP that is a living document, designed to be useful and used. It is easy to write an AUP to sit in a file cabinet and show to bureaucrats when they want to make sure you have one, but it is more important to create something that you can use, perhaps a framework for all Internet safety and digital citizenship education.

Each time an assignment or activity uses the Internet, you can refer back to the AUP as guidance for how to behave. You might even write more specific rules for a specific assignment. Bud Hunt (2008) has an example of rules for a blogging activity reproduced in Box 8.1.

Box 8.1

Blogging Safety Rules
Bud Hunt

1. Please, no last names, school names or addresses.

2. Do not link to your personal blog/journal from your school blog; you might reveal information on there that you don't want to reveal on your school blog.

3. If you want to write your opinion on a topic, make sure you're not going to be offensive to anyone as you write it.

4. Always make sure you check over your post for spelling errors, grammar errors, and your use of words.

5. Never disrespect someone else in your blog, whether it's a person, an organization, or just a general idea. You don't want someone making a stab at what you are passionate about; don't do it to someone else.

6. Don't write about other people without permission; if you can't get their permission, use first names only. Never share someone else's last name.

7. Watch your language! We're not at home, we are at school, this has to be at least remotely professional looking.

8. Make sure things you write about are factual. Don't be posting about things that aren't true.

9. Keep it education-oriented. That means that you probably shouldn't discuss your plans for the weekend.

Source: www.budtheteacher.com/wiki/index.php?title=Blogging_Rules
Used with permission.

As you can see, the rules in Box 8.1 are specific to blogging, but many of them any of them apply more generally. You might have a general set of rules relating, for example, to not putting personal information online. Hunt's rules 1, 2, and 6 in the context of blogging (see Box 8.1) might refer to the broader rules for students using the Internet. Similar guidelines for blogs, podcasts, and wikis—Self-Publishing and Social Media Guidelines: Pupils—can be found at http://edubuzz.pbworks.com/w/page/11239900/socialmediapupil.

Interacting online is becoming a natural part of what children do inside school and outside school. Working with them to be responsible digital citizens is an important part of helping them to mature. (See, for example, Andy Affleck's piece, Box 8.3 later in this chapter, in which he shares his thinking about using technology and social media with his children.)

Instructional Technology Coordinator of St. Vrain Valley School District in Longmont, Colorado, Bud Hunt, author of Blogging Safety Rules (Box 8.1), related to me how his school district has moved away from the idea that an acceptable use policy (AUP) as a separate concept from a general behavior policy. He said, "Our network is our 51st campus." Hunt's point is that acceptable use isn't restricted to how we use technology but is about how we interact with others. The administrators at St. Vrain Valley are not trying to put out a dos and don'ts list of technology (e.g., chat rooms are bad, but blogs are good); instead, they're trying to help students become responsible digital citizens.

The St. Vrain Valley School District has recrafted its policies related to technology into four documents: a policy on Technology, Access and Digital Communication (EHC); a complete legal policy on network use, titled St. Vrain Valley School District Terms, Conditions and Responsible Use Guidelines (EHC-R); a signature form for staff members to acknowledge their understanding of the policy, Responsible Use Guidelines for Technology, Access and Digital Communications (Staff) (EHC-E-1); and a student version of the policy, Student Responsible Use Guidelines for Technology, Access and Digital Communications (EHC-E-2). All of these documents can be found at www.stvrain.k12.co.us/policies/E by referencing the specific documents' codes in parentheses.

The policy on Technology, Access and Digital Communication (EHC) begins with this statement of philosophy:

> The Board is committed to connecting students and staff with each other and with resources around the world for improved collaboration and fast access to current information. Similarly, the Board is committed to providing access to information and expert resources for all of our students. Our students and staff both consume and create

information, and it is the job of the District to provide safe and reliable opportunities and spaces for students and staff to do both.

This statement of the district's philosophy is a powerful reminder that we are not dealing simply with technology but with "connecting students and staff with each other and with resources around the world for improved collaboration and fast access to current information." We must move beyond the model of education where technology is separate from the rest of education and online behavior is separate from being a responsible person in general. The details of etiquette might be different (LOL is appropriate in some contexts and not others), but the goals of learning and the human responsibilities are the same.

Every school or district needs a blanket AUP, which might include some legalese, but that is not going to help a fourth grader understand appropriate behavior. That is why schools need a document for students and possibly different documents for different grade levels. The document should be something the students can understand and use.

For the student document, the St. Vrain Valley School District has chosen to write a set of guidelines at a fifth grade reading level so all students can understand it (see Box 8.2).

Box 8.2

Student Responsible Use Guidelines for Technology, Access, and Digital Communication

St. Vrain Valley School District RE-1J

The St. Vrain Valley School District offers students access to computers and the Internet to support the District vision and mission. In order to provide open access to the resources, tools and equipment we believe are essential to teaching and learning, it is important that users understand their responsibilities and conduct themselves as responsible learners at all times. Listed below are guidelines that outline responsible use.

(Continued)

I will:

- Keep private information private. (My password and identity are mine and not to be shared.)

- Treat others with respect, both online and offline.

- Report anyone who tries to use the computer to hurt or harass me to a teacher or other adult.

- Strive to be a responsible digital citizen.

- Encourage others to be good digital citizens.

- Have appropriate conversations in all my interactions with others.

- Tell adults when someone makes me uncomfortable.

- Use computers for school-related purposes.

- Credit my sources when I am using other people's information, images, or other material.

- Respect the work of other students and not try to copy, damage, or delete their work.

- Follow District policies, rules, and regulations.

- Ask for permission before connecting my own devices to the District network.

- Take care of District computer equipment.

I will not:

- Read another student's private communications without permission.

- Use improper language or pictures.

- Use communication tools to spread lies about others.

- Pretend to be someone else online.

- Give out my full name, password, address, or any other personal information to someone I don't know.

- Give out the full names and addresses of others.

- Send email to anyone who asks me not to.

- Look for, read, view, or copy inappropriate pictures or information.

- Load my own software on the District network to use at school, unless I have received permission.
- Try to get access to or make the computer or network do things not approved by my school and the District.

I understand:

- That sometimes my computer work may be lost and I should be careful to back up important work.
- That some things I read on the Internet may not be true.
- That the computers and network belong to the District and that using them is a privilege, not a right.
- That the computers, network, and printers may not work every day.
- That it is my responsibility to make sure that any devices I use on the District network are approved.
- That the things that I do using a school computer or network are not private and that my teachers and District staff may review my work and activities at any time.
- That it is my responsibility to read and abide by the terms and conditions of Board Policy EHC-R and all revisions.

Consequences for misuse:

- I might not be allowed to use the computers or the District network if I break these rules.
- I may be suspended or expelled from school if I act irresponsibly.

(Approved March 9, 2005; Reviewed April 23, 2008; Revised May 12, 2010)

Source: St. Vrain Valley School District RE-1J, Longmont, Colorado; www.stvrain.k12.co.us/policies/E/EHC-E-2.pdf
Used with permission.

The goal is to have a document that is used and usable. It has shifted from a series of Thou Shalt Nots to three sections: I Will, I Will Not, and I Understand. The goal is to set higher expectations and not assume the worst. The policy is no longer an acceptable use policy but "Student Responsible Use Guidelines." The change in wording is subtle, but it relates to the change in philosophy of presenting a set of positive expectations. By starting with *I will*, these guidelines set a positive tone, asking students to live up to high standards.

Although the guidelines end with the possibility that access to resources might be taken away, Hunt agrees that this cannot be a first option. If we are serious about integrating networked resources into the curriculum, it is no longer an option to cut off access any more than we would say, "You've been bad so you can no longer have a pencil and textbook.

As for safety curricula, Hunt suggests that the best Internet safety is to teach responsible citizenship. He is partial to the Generation YES (GenYES) program (http://genyes.org) and the Common Sense Media Programs (www.commonsensemedia.org/educators). The GenYES program focuses on integrating technology into the curriculum, learning appropriate behaviors as part of real learning activities. The Digital Literacy and Citizenship Curriculum from Common Sense Media guides students through lessons about safety and security as well as digital citizenship. The curriculum is divided into courses for students in Grades K–5, 6–8, and 9–12; a sample, downloadable lesson for students in Grades 6–8, Cyberbullying: Crossing the Line, is available (www.commonsensemedia. org/educators/curriculum). Common Sense Media also offers a Parent Media Education Program. The goal of both programs is to engage students in discussions about real issues they will encounter.

Many other safety curricula are available to schools and teachers, so when choosing, try to steer away from fear-based curricula and look for curricula that highlight the positive uses of technology and how students can benefit from being safe and responsible. Some lessons in digital citizenship might be separate lessons, but every time technology is used, some piece of safe and responsible use can be incorporated. When interacting with others, students can be reminded of the importance of being polite. When accessing information, students can learn about plagiarism and resource evaluation. When accessing media online, students can learn about copyright. When posting information online, students can learn about limiting the personal information they give out, as well as how that information can have long-term consequences. As various issues come up, teachers can use them as positive teachable moments, adding clarification of real-life values to students' learning. This kind of guidance, by trusted and caring adults, will help students become better digital citizens.

In Box 8.3: When Should We Introduce Social Media to Kids? Andy Affleck writes, "many of the parents in my generation have no clue about appropriate online behavior." Affleck discusses social media and children, Facebook and his own child in particular, from a parent's perspective.

Box 8.3

When Should We Introduce Social Media to Kids?

Andy Affleck

When my son was in third grade, he attended a Waldorf school where modern technology and media—TVs, computers, mobile phones, video games, and so on—are severely restricted. My wife and I embraced that idea while simultaneously feeing a little uncomfortable about it.

On the one hand, kids need to be kids and there should be no rush to have them grow up and be exposed to more-adult things. I also came away from my time at the Harvard Graduate School of Education's Technology in Education program with the firm belief that computers in education make more sense at older ages than at younger ages. Kids need the hands-on, get-your-fingers-dirty aspects of childhood. All the constructivist (and constructionist) theories and tools can't hold a candle to actual mucking about with objects in the real world.

On the other hand, adults use technology constantly, from the iPhone and iPad to the Mac, and we spend time on Twitter and Facebook, among many other online services. So it has become harder to stick to this viewpoint over the years, not because of improvements to educational technology, but rather because of the continuing insinuation of advanced technology into everyday life and the rapid growth of social media. And that raises the question of when a child is old enough to be allowed to use the same technological products and services that we adults do.

My son, now 10 years old, wants a Facebook account. He wants the restrictions to chat removed on his FreeRealms account. He's starting to be bothered by the limits in interactions in Webkinz, and he wants to video chat with his friends on Skype. Also, he wants to make digital things. He wants to write games to share with his friends on the web, he wants to become a YouTube star (so far, I'm helping him do movie reviews) and he wants to write, film,

(Continued)

edit, and score a movie (I signed him up for a mini-camp at the local Apple Store to get him started).

I'm beginning to adjust my thinking about what technology he should be allowed to use. The content creation and publishing tools don't bother me much—they have only recently become usable by kids. But the social media question is harder. His generation will be far more connected than mine is. Why should we hold off on introducing him to that world? It will play such a significant role in his life that it seems to me his education should begin sooner. If he is to be truly successful in the world when he comes of age, he should be armed to the teeth with knowledge and skills.

Of course, the big issue is his age. He and his peers are too young to navigate the eddies and swirls of the social media stream. You read about the horror stories of young people getting online and not being able to deal with the bullying and pressures that exist out there. Alarmist pieces like "Facebook pressure: The horrifying week I spent spying on my 11-year-old daughter['s Facebook page]" (www.dailymail.co.uk/femail/article-1289070/Facebook-pressure-The-horrifying-week-I-spent-spying-11-year-old-daughter.html) scare parents into clamping down on social media use when, in fact, the author of that very article actually happens on the solution: parental supervision.

When our children go out into the real world at this age, they never do so alone. We parents accompany them. I go with my son when he needs to go to the store. I take him to his play dates. I take him to his scouting and karate events. Or he goes with my wife or another parent. Pre-teens are almost never left alone without adult supervision, to keep them safe and to ensure nothing bad happens. Kids at this age are not good at seeing consequences to their actions, and they do many ill-considered things.

So it's our job as parents to protect our children and to keep things from getting out of hand. It is our voices that tell them not to get too close to the campfire or to stay off the rocks so no one falls. It is we who tell them to look both ways when crossing the street, to eat their vegetables, to turn off the TV and read a book, to go to bed now, to not treat their friend that way, and to answer the telephone politely. We tell them when to say please and thank you so they learn at least the form of manners, even if their understanding of why manners are important won't come for years. We pay attention to their social interactions to help prevent them from becoming bullies or complete introverts. We guide them and teach them how to work within our society.

Parents do all these things in the real world, but at the same time many tell their children that they cannot go online. They prohibit all things online because they are scared of the bullying and the predators out there. And they do this even though online predation is a vastly overblown worry (www. nytimes.com/2009/01/14/technology/Internet/14cyberweb.html) and research has shown that bullying is still more an offline problem (www.zephoria.org/ thoughts/archives/2010/06/24/risky-behaviors-and-online-safety-a-2010-literature-review.html) than an online one.

Parents also latch onto things like Facebook's age limits, which restrict accounts to those who are at least 13 years old. It's an easy crutch, so they either lean on it or end up inadvertently teaching their kids that lying about their age is OK to get them in early. Ironically, the age restriction is not there to protect kids, but rather exists as the way these sites handle COPPA, the Children's Online Privacy Protection Act (www.coppa.org). See "How COPPA Fails Parents, Educators, Youth" for an explanation (http://dmlcentral.net/ blog/danah-boyd/how-coppa-fails-parents-educators-youth).

But all of these knee-jerk reactions assume that we are going to hand over the computer and walk away.

Instead, we should start to walk our kids into this online world just as we walk them into the real world. Let them get online but supervise them. Allow them to start exploring and learning how the online world works but stay with them on the journey until they can go alone, the same way we already do this in the real world. (At the same time, we need to recognize how immersive and compelling this online world can be and set sensible limits. Children should still run outside and play with real toys, not spend all of their time online with virtual friends.)

If you see bullying in the real world, you inform the parent of the offending child and hope they will do something about it. If you see bullying online, you can do the same thing. And if the other parent fails to address the problem in the real world, you can usually escalate the complaint to an authority figure—

(Continued)

a bus driver, teacher, or principal. That's not possible online, but in the virtual world, you can block the bully from contacting your kid entirely, which isn't possible in the real world. If your own child acts inappropriately, you are there to stop it and explain how social networks work, or at least how they should work. In short, you can teach your kids how to act in polite online society, just as you teach them to navigate social situations in the real world.

Of course, the fallacy with this approach is that many of the parents in my generation have no clue about appropriate online behavior. Luckily, most of what's necessary can be accomplished merely by sitting with your children as they explore online, so you are there to correct or guide. I wish there were an online course for parents to teach them what they need to know to do their jobs correctly in the new media space. And I also wish our schools would take up the challenge and find a way to add social networking tools to their curricula so that children learn to use them in a smart, effective, and ethical manner.

As regards my own family, I am not saying that I will let my son lie and get a Facebook account. I do still believe that we must consider age appropriateness. He is just learning how to use the phone to call his friends (we still have to remind him to be polite to adults, tell them who he is when he calls, and things like that), he can't type that well yet, and, frankly, he's only 10. There's plenty of time. (That said, we've just learned of a new site called Togetherville that piggybacks on Facebook and provides some level of access with full parental supervision. We will be exploring it as a possible bridge to Facebook when he is older.)

But my reasons for holding him back from at least the social media side of things stem not from fear but rather from a belief that he is not sufficiently mature or socially adept yet. I believe he will reach that state long before he's 13, but I'll deal with that conundrum then. Meanwhile, he can create all the content he wants, start his own blog, and more. And as he does and when he's ready for social networking, I'll be there to guide him, just as I am out in the real world.

Source: Originally published in TidBITS, October 4, 2010, available at http://tidbits.com/article/11633

Used with permission.

Conclusion

The Internet has issues, but so does the real world. We don't respond to problems in the real world by locking our children behind closed doors. Instead, we guide them and gradually give them more freedom, as we help them to understand how to communicate with strangers, treat people respectfully, deal with money, talk about sex, and so on. We shield them from some things when they are young and open them to the possibilities and the problems more and more as they get older.

The same is true for the Internet. Children need some protection and shielding, and they need a lot of guidance and understanding to help them learn appropriate behavior. If our goal is simply to keep them safe in the short term, we might be able to do that with locks and filters. But our goals are to motivate them, educate them, and help them mature into responsible adults and lifelong learners. This requires that we use many of the tools that the Internet makes available while providing constraints, supervision, and guidance. It is easier to shut everything out, but if we do, we are giving up on our larger goals. That means that it is our responsibility to learn about the problems our students might encounter, teach them in advance how to avoid those problems, and teach them in real time when they encounter the problems anyway. Effective education and effective policies will help our students learn and grow.

Exercises

1. Create an acceptable use policy for your classroom. Be sure that it is appropriate for your students—with language they can understand, a positive tone, and appropriate consequences (possibly tied to the school's general behavior system). If you are currently in the classroom, consider working with your students to have them help you write the policy.

2. Review some of the cyberbullying resources in the References section of this chapter, particularly Willard (2007b), and write a plan of action for your school for creating effective policies and procedures to address cyberbullying.

References

Burbules, N. C., & Callister, T. A., Jr. (2000). *Watch IT: The risks and promises of information technologies for education*. Boulder, CO: Westview Press.

Federal Communication Commission. (2009). Children's Internet Protection Act [Web page]. Retrieved from http://www.fcc.gov/guides/childrens-internet-protection-act

Federal Communication Commission. (2011, August 10). Schools and libraries universal service support mechanism: A national broadband plan for our future. Retrieved from http://hraunfoss.fcc.gov/edocs_public/attachmatch/FCC-11-125A1.pdf

Federal Trade Commission (2010). Net cetera: Chatting with kids about being online. Available from http://onguardonline.gov/articles/0028-cyberbullying

Hunt, B. (2008). Blogging rules. Retrieved January 3, 2011, from http://www.budtheteacher.com/wiki/index.php?title=Blogging_Rules

Internet Safety Technical Taskforce. (2008, December 31). Enhancing child safety and online technologies: Final report of the Internet Safety Technical Task Force to the Multi-State Working Group on Social Networking of State Attorneys General of the United States. Retrieved January 5, 2011, from http://cyber.law.harvard.edu/sites/cyber.law.harvard.edu/files/ISTTF_Final_Report.pdf

Khadaroo, S. T. (2010, October 8). Report: One-third of US teens are victims of cyberbullying. *The Christian Science Monitor*. Retrieved from http://www.csmonitor.com/USA/Society/2010/1008/Report-One-third-of-US-teens-are-victims-of-cyberbullying

Levinson, M. (2010). *From fear to Facebook: One school's journey*. Eugene, OR: International Society for Technology in Education.

National Public Radio. (1997, September 12). Web and smut filters [Radio broadcast]. Retrieved from http://www.npr.org/templates/story/story.php?storyId=1028056

Tarbox, K. (2000). *Katie.com: My story*. New York, NY: Dutton Adult Division, Penguin Books.

Warlick, D. (2008). School AUP 2.0 [Dynamic document]. Retrieved January 3, 2011, from http://landmark-project.com/aup20/pmwiki.php

Weinberg, A. M. (1966). Can technology replace social engineering? *Bulletin of the Atomic Scientists, 12*(10): 4–8.

Willard, N. (n.d.). *Techno-Panic & 21st century education: Make sure Internet safety messaging does not undermine education for the future.* Retrieved February 9, 2012, from http://www.csriu.org/documents/documents/Techno-Panic_001.pdf

Willard, N. (2003). *Safe and responsible use of the Internet: A guide for educators.* Eugene, OR: Responsible Netizen Institute. Retrieved from http://csriu.org/onlinedocs/pdf/srui/chapters/part2/chapterII1.pdf

Willard, N. (2007a). *Cyberbullying and cyberthreats: Responding to the challenge of online social aggression, threats, and distress.* Champaign, IL: Research Press.

Willard, N. (2007b). *Educator's guide to cyberbullying and cyberthreats.* Available from the Center for Safe and Responsible Use of the Internet, http://www.cyberbully.org/documents; http://www.cyberbully.org/cyberbully/docs/cbcteducator.pdf

Willard, N. (2010). Cyber secure schools in a Web 2.0 world: Creating change in technology adoption, effective Internet use management, Web 2.0 in schools, legal issues. Available from the Center for Safe and Responsible Internet Use, http://www.csriu.org; http://csriu.cerizmo.com/categories/1125-cyber-secure-schools-in-a-web-2-0-world

CHAPTER NINE

Basics of Web Design and HTML

When I teach students to use HTML to create web pages, I always get asked why. Although I am tempted to respond with, "Eat your vegetables; they are good for you," that is not the reason why. I do not expect most teachers to use HTML in any significant way. Plenty of web page creation tools, such as KompoZer (http://www.kompozer.net) and Adobe Dream Weaver (http://www.adobe.com/products/dreamweaver.html) as well as blog and wiki tools are available, so most teachers will rarely, if ever, need to use HTML. Some teachers might enjoy creating web pages and find HTML a powerful tool, but they are the exception. This chapter is for those exceptional teachers; it will get you started so you can easily explore more in-depth coverage on websites, such as Draac.com (http://www.draac.com), or books, such as *Head First HTML with CSS & XHTML* by Elisabeth Freeman and Eric Freeman (2006).

But what about the rest of you? If you don't hope to be an HTML geek and haven't stopped reading this chapter yet, why should you read on? Here are four reasons:

1. The web is ruled by HTML. Just about any web page that you see is built with HTML.

2. Because of number 1, HTML code pops up in unlikely places.

3. Sometimes the tools don't work right, and tweaking the HTML is the easiest or only way to do what you want.

4. As much as we would like to use WYSIWYG (what-you-see-is-what-you-get) tools or what I call word-processor-like tools, web pages differ from word-processing documents in important ways, and understanding HTML will help you understand those differences and help you use the WYSIWYG tools more effectively.

Have you ever looked at the source of a web page? Go to any page in your browser and look for the Source (or View Source or Page Source) command (sometimes in the View menu, often available by right-clicking on a page). One of the first three lines you will see is almost certainly <html>:

<html>

This is the HTML tag, indicating that what follows is an HTML document. It might include CSS (Cascading Style Sheets) or JavaScript or embedded flash, but at its heart, it is HTML.

At times, you will see HTML pop up on your screen when some kind of error occurs, but you might also see it when you use tools. For example, Blogger (http://www.blogger.

com), Google's blogging tool, has a mode to edit blog posts in HTML (click on the Edit HTML tab at the top of the edit window). You can choose that mode, but I have found that I am sometimes put in the mode without my choosing. There are still some tools available (such as a linking tool), but if you're not familiar with HTML, you might be surprised at what you get:

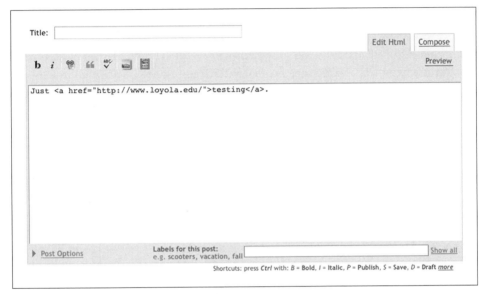

Figure 9.1 HTML at http://www.blogger.com.

The link (Figure 9.1) is created with an HTML tag. Clicking on the Compose tab will switch back to a WYSIWYG view, but simply knowing that the <a> tag is a link will help you understand what has happened.

Now, recognizing anomalies is helpful, but you gain great power when you realize that you can use HTML to your advantage. For example, imagine that you wanted your link to open in a new window or tab, rather than taking the current window to the linked location. Without HTML, Blogger does not give you that option.

With HTML, simply adding **target="new"** to the <a> tag makes it happen.

> **target="new"**

And if you didn't know that, but you had a basic grasp of HTML, you could search for this solution and easily understand how to implement it. Without HTML, you might find the solution, but you wouldn't know what to do with **target="new"**.

The most compelling reason to start your web authoring with a basic understanding of HTML is that it will help you understand the WYSIWYG tools that make web page creation almost as easy as word processing. I have had many teachers tell me that they had had great difficulty with WYSIWYG tools. After spending a couple of hours learning HTML, they found that the WYSIWYG tools made perfect sense. The explanation is simple. WYSIWYG tools behave like word processors. The ways in which web pages are like word-processing documents are the same ways that WYSIWYG tools make perfect sense. The ways that web pages are different from word processing documents are the ways that WYSIWYG tools are difficult to understand. A basic understanding of HTML gives you the power to understand both the word-processing-like features of the WYSIWYG tools, as well as the features that are different from word processors. The result is that learning HTML means that you need little or no instruction to use a WYSIWYG web page creation tool with ease.

What You Need to Create Web Pages with HTML

All you need to get started making web pages is a simple word processor and a browser. You can use any word processor to edit your HTML and any browser to view your completed web pages.

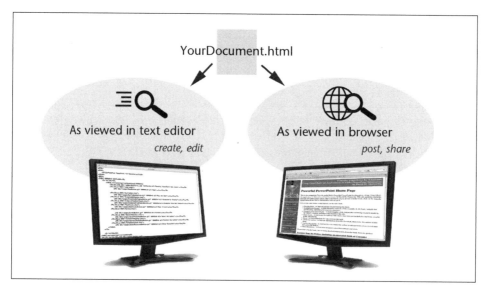

Figure 9.2 One document, two views.

The keys are to save your file as a text file and give it a name ending in **.htm** or **.html**. Simple word processors, like NotePad or WordPad in Windows and TextEdit on a Macintosh work very well. More complex word processors, like Microsoft Word, tend to recognize that you are making a web page and try to take over the process, so I don't recommend them. Fortunately, NotePad and WordPad are standard on Windows, and TextEdit is standard on a Macintosh running OS X (before OS X, Macs used SimpleText or TeachText).

The most difficult part of this process is a conceptual one. You need to understand that you are going to create one document, but you are going to open it with two different applications. You will view and edit the HTML code using a word processor, and you will view the web page as it will appear on the web through a browser. Always remember that whether you are in a word processor or a browser, you are looking at the same document; you are just looking at it through two different lenses (Figure 9.2).

Four Steps to Creating an HTML Document

There are four things you will want to do when creating an HTML document:

1. Create a new document and save it for the first time.

2. View your new document in a browser (Internet Explorer, Firefox, etc.) for the first time.

3. Edit your document and view the changes in your browser.

4. Open an old document in your word processor for editing and in your browser for viewing.

None of these steps are difficult, but each is extremely important if you want to get your web pages to work.

Step 1: Create Your Document and Save It

In order to create a new document, you must open your word processor. Full-featured word processors are not always the best choice because of auto-formatting features that will reinterpret your text and otherwise be too smart for their own good.

When saving a file, you must pay attention to three important things:

■ What type of file is it?

■ Where is the file going?

■ What is the file called?

Creating Your File

Much of what you need to do, particularly the type of file you'll create, depends on the program you are using. Notepad only saves text files, so you don't have to worry about the file type at all. WordPad and TextEdit can save text files as well as rich text files, so the file type will be an issue.

First you'll find the program you want to use. WordPad and NotePad are Windows applications that come with the operating system. They generally can be found in the Start Menu by choosing Programs and Accessories. TextEdit is a Macintosh program, and it generally can be found in the Applications folder on your hard drive.

Creating a Place for Your File

Before starting to create a web page, it is a good idea to create a folder. You will put all files related to the web page or website in that folder. When you decide to move the web page to another location on your computer, to a flash drive, to a CD, to another computer, or to a server on the web, it is critical that you keep all the files together, so it is best to move the entire folder, not individual files. This is one difference between most word-processing documents and web pages. Most word-processing documents are self-contained; that is, if you have the file (such as a .docx file), you have the entire document. But HTML is only text; it does not include pictures or sounds or videos. That doesn't mean that web pages don't contain pictures or sounds or videos. When you look at a page on the web, it seems like the pictures and sounds and videos are all parts of the page. But those nontext elements are actually stored in separate files. HTML provides a link to those files, so the browser can use its magic to make them look like they are part of the page. If the HTML file and the other files get separated, the sounds and pictures and videos won't show up on the page. So, the most important thing to remember is to make a folder, put everything in it, and keep everything in it.

If you are using Windows, once you have created your folder and started your simple word processor, you can type your HTML document. If you are using a Mac, see this chapter's section titled "Using TextEdit on a Macintosh" for instructions about adjusting the settings in TextEdit before you can type your document, and then return here. Later in this chapter, we'll review some basic HTML tags, so you'll know what to type. For now, you could start with this sample starter web page:

```
<html>
    <head>
            <title>My Web Page</title>
    </head>
    <body>
            <p>This is my first Web page.</p>
    </body>
</html>
```

Naming and Saving Your File

Now go to your File menu and choose Save. You will save to a folder. If you created a folder for your web page, be sure to save the file into that folder. (See Figure 9.3.)

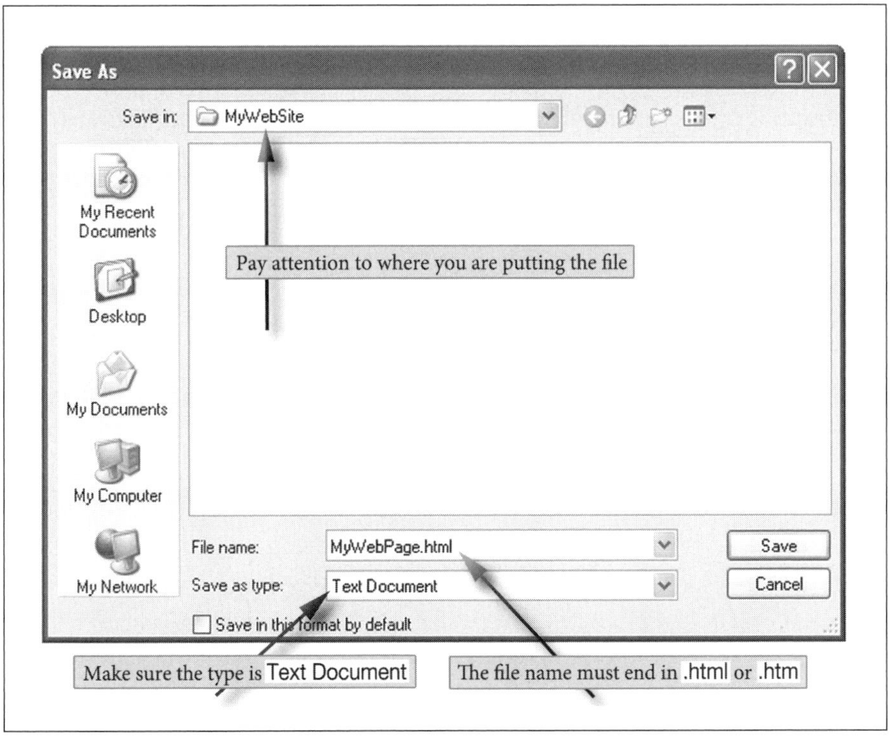

Figure 9.3 Saving your document: Paying attention to where it's going, what it's called, and what type of file it is.

Make sure that you are saving to your folder. If you forgot to create a folder, click on the folder icon with a starburst to create a new folder and save there. Next, make sure that the "Save as type" is set to Text Document (if you are using Notepad, don't worry about the type). Finally, type a file name using the following rules:

1. Only use numbers and letters (avoid spaces and punctuation).

2. End the file name with **.html** or **.htm**.

For the first rule, some characters besides numbers and letters will work, and some will not. It is hard to remember whether, for example, a slash will work and a dash will not or vice versa, so I recommend simplifying the name and sticking with letters and numbers. I also recommend avoiding spaces in file names. They will work, but sometimes browsers turn a space into *%20*—and you probably don't want that in your file name. The *.htm* or *.html* at the end tells the computer that this is a web page.

Using TextEdit on a Macintosh

If you use Macintosh OS X, you will have access to TextEdit. This simple word processor has many of the same features as WordPad for the PC, including the ability to save and read RTF (rich text format) files and interpret HTML commands. In order to ensure that your document is created as a regular, ordinary, everyday text file (as opposed to a rich text file), you will have to do the following:

■ Open TextEdit (probably in the Applications folder of your hard drive).

■ From the TextEdit menu, choose Preferences.

■ Under the New Document tab, change Format to Plain Text and check the box for Wrap to Page.

■ Under the Open and Save tab, "When saving a file," uncheck the box for "Add '.txt' extension to plain text files."

■ And "When opening a file," check the box for "Ignore rich text commands in HTML files."

Once you have set up these settings (Figure 9.4), you will have to close the current TextEdit document and open a new one (or quit TextEdit and start it up again). This is necessary because the New Document preferences are for a new document and won't apply to any document that has already been created, including the blank one that opened when you first started TextEdit.

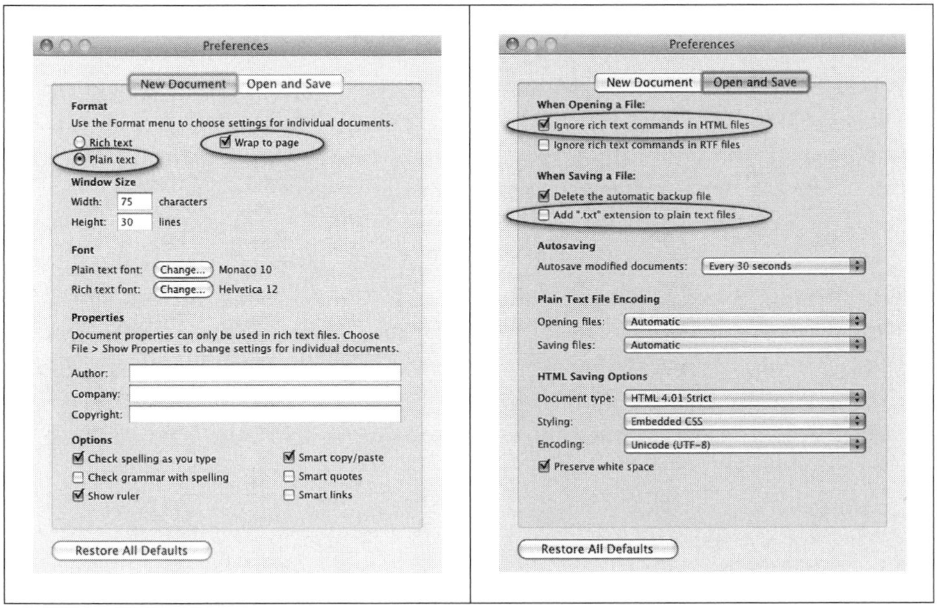

Figure 9.4 Settings for TextEdit on the Mac: New Document (left) and Open and Save (right).

With these settings, you won't have to worry about saving a file as a Text File; you just have to worry about the file location and the file name. Everything else will work in basically the same way, regardless of what simple word processor you are using.

Step 2: View Your Document in a Browser

Once you have created your document, you will want to view it in your browser (e.g., Internet Explorer, Safari, or Firefox). Because you will want to go back and forth between editing your document (in the word processor) and viewing it (in the browser), you will not want to close the document; you will want to minimize or hide it. On a Macintosh, you can simply go to the TextEdit menu and choose Hide TextEdit (or Hide whatever word processor you are using), or simply click on the yellow button to minimize the window. In Windows, you can minimize the current application by clicking on the line in the upper right hand corner (you have three buttons: a line for minimize, two overlapping squares or one big square to change the size of the window, and an X to close the window). Choose the line to minimize.

There are two ways to open your file in the browser. The easiest way is to find the file itself (in Finder or Windows Explorer, not in any application). It will be in the folder you created to save all your files. Then, right-click on the file (control-click if you use a one-button mouse), choose Open With, and pick your browser.

Alternatively, you can open your browser in whatever way you normally do this (from the Start menu, from the Macintosh Dock, from a big *e* on your desktop, etc.). Once your browser is open, you will need to find the file that you have just created and saved. In the File menu, you should choose Open or Open File or something similar, depending on which version of which browser you are using. (If you are using Internet Explorer 7 for Windows or later, you might find that you don't have any menus; if this is the case, right-click in a blank area near the top of the screen, just below where the URL is showing, and choose Menu Bar from the vertical flyout menu.) At this point, you will either already be in a standard Open File dialogue box, or you will need to do something (probably click on a button marked Browse) to get into a standard Open File dialogue box. You will then navigate through your computer to find the file in the place you saved it. Once you find the file, click on it, and click Open or Open File. In Windows, you probably have to click OK at this point, and you should see the file in your browser as it will look on the web.

If you typed the HTML code for the sample starter page (p. 193), you should see two things: In the title bar at the top of the window, you should see *My Web Page*; in the main part of the page, you should see the sentence *This is my first Web page*.

There are three likely things that can go wrong:

- You could not find the file.
- You found the file, but it does not look right.
- You found the file and it will not open.

If you could not find the file at all, you either forgot where you put it, or you did not save it with the **.html** or **.htm** extension. If the latter is the case, you will have to use Save As in the word processor to save it again with the proper extension.

If you found the file, but it does not look right, that is par for the course. That is why you will have to edit (see the next section). If it looks almost identical to the way it looked in the word processor, including all the HTML tags, you probably did not save it with the **.html** or **.htm** extension, and you will have to use Save As in the word processor to save it again with the proper extension.

If it looks like a bunch of gobbledygook or has your text along with a bunch of extra characters with percent signs and slashes, you probably did not save it as a Text File (you probably saved it as a Rich Text File), and you will have to use Save As in the word processor to save it again as a Text File.

If you found the file and it will not open, you probably gave it a bad name. Some systems will have trouble opening some file names, especially those with spaces or unacceptable characters in them. If this is the case, try using Save As in the word processor to save it again with a simpler name (just letters and numbers and ending in **.html** or **.htm**).

Step 3: Edit Your Document and View Changes in the Browser

If you found the document in the browser, and it looks something like a web page, you are doing very well. Now, you will want to make changes to the document and view the changes in the browser. First, switch back to the word processor, and then follow a simple four-step process.

If you followed the above directions and hid or minimized the word processor (and did not close it), you can easily switch back to it either by choosing it from the task bar or dock. Now make whatever changes you want to make. For example, add another sentence so the text says, *This is my first web page. I hope you like it.* Then, perform the following four steps:

1. Save the file. Go to the File menu and choose Save. That's it! You have already told the computer where the file is going and what it is called, so you don't have to tell it again.

2. Save the file as a text document. Some programs (such as WordPad) will insist that you confirm that you want this to be a Text Document every time you save it. If your program asks when you try to save the file, just tell it you want a Text Document. If it doesn't ask, it is automatically saving it as a Text Document.

3. Switch to the browser. Select the browser either on the dock (Macintosh) or in the task bar (PC).

4. Click on the Refresh or Reload button. The browser only looks at the page when you load it. It doesn't know that changes have been made. Refreshing tells the browser to go look at the page again.

All these steps are necessary. Any changes you make will not be in the file that is on disk until you save the file (step 1). We want to make sure it is still a text document (step 2). You need to be in the browser to see the file as it will look on the web (step 3). The browser will not automatically read the changes until you tell it to do so (step 4); until then, it will still be showing you the old version of the file.

Step 4: Open an Old Document

Once you are done, you will close up all your programs and go away. At some point, you will want to come back and edit the document some more and view it in your browser. Because you need to view it two different ways (in the word processor and in the browser), you can't simply double-click on the file and expect it to open in both views. Depending on your computer's settings and operating system, when you double click on a file, it might open in the program that created it, or it might open in the program that is associated with the file extension (in this case, the **.htm** or **.html** will have it open with the browser).

As with opening the document in the browser for the first time, there are two ways to open the document (both in the word processor and browser). The easy way is to locate the file in Finder or Windows (that is, not choosing Open from the File menu from within an application). Once you see the icon for the file, right-click on the file (hold down the control key and click on a one-button mouse). You should get a fly-out menu that includes Open With. On a Windows computer, choose WordPad (or NotePad or whatever simple word processor you are using) from the Open With list. If WordPad or NotePad does not appear on your Open With list, choose Default Programs from that list and either click on the arrow next to "other programs" or click on the Browse button. On a Mac, choose TextEdit. Next minimize the file (do not close it) and repeat the right-click and Open With, but this time, choose your browser from the Open With list (Safari, Firefox, Internet Explorer, etc.).

Alternatively, you can do this from within the applications. To open the file in your word processor, start the word processor (as you did to create a new document), and go to the file menu and choose open. You will be presented with the standard Open Dialogue box, but you might not be able to see your file (if you are in Windows). You might have to choose what type of file you want to be able to see. If, for example, you are using WordPad, it will automatically be looking for "Files of type" Word for Windows (*.doc), and it will not show you **.html** or **.htm** files. Other word processors might automatically be looking for "Files of type" Text (*.txt). Find the choice for "Files of type" and choose All Documents (*.*). You can now go to the location where you saved the file, and you should be able to see it and open it normally.

You should now have the document open in both your simple word processor and your browser, so you can easily switch to the word processor to make changes and switch to the browser to view those changes as they would appear on the web. But before we get to some serious editing, we might want to verify that we have the same file open in both the browser and the word processor. It is unlikely, but possible, that you opened a different file (or different version of the same file) in the browser from the one you opened in the word processor. Verifying that you have the same file is easy. You will want to make a simple, hard-to-mess-up change to your document and then view that change in the browser. Add another sentence to the text so it now reads, *This is my first Web page. I hope you like it. I did it all by myself.* Follow the four steps (from p. 197) to view the changes in your browser.

If you see the changes in your browser, you are ready to tackle some HTML tags. If you don't, close everything down and try again.

POINTS TO REMEMBER

- Never save your web page from the browser; only save it using the simple word processor you used to create it. Just use the browser to view it.

- Save everything in the same folder, including all HTML and picture files.

- When posting on a server, move the folder and all its contents to the server.

- Only use .jpg, .gif, or .png image formats.

- Use simple file names (only letters and numbers ending in .html or .htm—no spaces or hyphens or slashes or other special characters).

- Don't open your page with a fancy word processor (like Microsoft Word); it will only mess things up.

HTML Tags

Tags are the commands that tell the computer what to do. If you want text to be large and bold, for example, you use the tag to tell the computer to make the text large and bold. Tags are enclosed in angle brackets. The tag to make text large and bold is h1, so it appears in your file as **<h1>**.

Most tags have an open tag and a close tag. Everything in between the open and close tag is affected by the tag. A close tag looks the same as the open tag, except that it begins with a forward slash.

Here's an example with an open tag and close tag:

> **<h1>This is my big heading</h1>**
> **This is not part of the big heading.**

The words *This is my big heading* are between the **<h1>** tag and the **</h1>** tag, so they are going to be big and bold. If you forget the close tag, the browser won't know when to stop making things big and bold, so you might end up with everything in your document being big and bold.

Keep in mind that any formatting that you do in the word processor (centering, bold, tabs, fonts, sizes, etc.) will be ignored by the computer when you look at the web page in the browser. You must use the HTML tags to do all of your formatting.

Parameters

Some tags also have parameters associated with them. Parameters give the tag more information. For example, the table tag tells the computer that you want to have a table, and it can have several parameters that tell the computer more information about the table. For example, you can tell the computer how wide you want the table to be:

> **<table width="100%">**
>
> ...
>
> **</table>**

This tells the computer that you want a table that takes up 100% of the width of the screen. Notice that the **</table>** tag does not need to include the parameters.

Basic Tags

Now you will learn a few basic tags that will help you make your pages look like real web pages and act like real web pages. You will learn how to add to your documents: paragraphs, headings, links, pictures, lists, and tables. This is simply a basic introduction. There are many more tags and parameters to learn, so I encourage you to use this chapter as a starting point and to explore some of the resources mentioned at the end of the chapter or any others to learn more.

Parts of an HTML Document

Let's take a look at the sample page we typed earlier:

```
<html>
    <head>
            <title>My Web Page</title>
    </head>
    <body>
            <p>This is my first Web page. I hope you like it.
            I made it all by myself.</p>
    </body>
</html>
```

You should notice that the document starts with the <html> tag and ends with the </html> tag. These always go at the beginning and end of a document, signifying that everything in between is the HTML document. If you leave either tag off, the browser will probably read the file just fine, but it is proper to put these tags at the beginning and end of your document.

Next, you should see two sections to the document: the HEAD and the BODY. The HEAD starts with the <head> tag and ends with the </head> tag. The BODY starts with the <body> tag and ends with the </body> tag. Generally, the last two lines of the document are the </body> and </html> tags.

The HEAD is reserved for behind-the-scenes information. There are special tags for keywords (to help search engines find your page) that can go in the HEAD. There are scripts (like JavaScript) and style commands (like CSS) that can go in the HEAD. These things might affect what you see on the page, but they don't, themselves, appear on the page. Anything that is to appear on the main part of the page goes in the BODY.

In our HEAD, we only have a TITLE. This is not the big bold information that goes at the top of the page. Instead, this is what goes in the title bar of the browser window (that small area at the very top of every window). In our page, between the <title> and </title> tags, we have *My Web Page*. Don't look for this in the body of the page (the main part of the screen), look for these words in the title bar.

Figure 9.5 shows how this page will look in the browser.

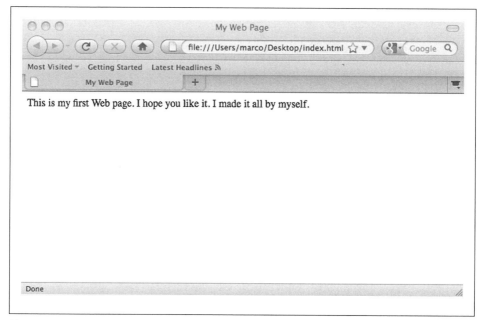

Figure 9.5 Sample starter web page viewed by browser.

Indentation

You might notice that the example indents certain lines in the HTML code. The computer does not care how you indent. However, as pages get more complicated, the HTML code is easier to read when you indent. For example, you will see in our code that the HEAD is indented from the <html> and </html> tags. This tells you, as you read your HTML code, that the HEAD is part of the HTML document. Likewise, the TITLE is indented from the <head> and </head> tags, indicating that the TITLE is part of the HEAD. Is this important? Not really. In fact, it will work just fine if you don't indent at all, and for the things above, you might choose not to bother indenting at all. When tags get more complex (such as lists and tables), indenting will help you understand what you mean to do (and make reading your own work easier), so you can get the code to do what you want.

QUOTATION MARKS

A smart word processor might change your straight quotation marks to *smart* quotation marks (that curve inward, ", or outward, "). Browsers will have a hard time with smart quotation marks that are used as part of tags (inside the angle brackets) so use a dumb word processor or turn off the autocorrect feature that turns straight quotes into smart quotes.

Capitals

Tags enclosed inside angle brackets can be typed with capital letters, lowercase letters, or any combination of capitals and lowercase letters. The spelling of the tag, however, must be correct: <hed> won't work; <heAD> will work. Most standards suggest that tags should be typed with all lowercase letters: <head>.

Paragraphs

You might notice that if you try to make paragraphs the way you do in a word processor (hitting Enter a couple of extra times or hitting tab at the beginning of the paragraph to indent), your formatting doesn't show up as a paragraph. All the text just runs together in one big block. The browser ignores all extra white space (more than one space, tab, or enter). If you want a new paragraph, you need a tag for that. In this case, the <p> tag:

> <p>This is my first paragraph. I hope you like it. I did it all by
> myself. If I hit the Enter key, it will be treated like a space so if
> I want a new paragraph, I have to use the p tag.</p>
> <p>This is my second paragraph. Because I used the proper tag,
> it will not be clumped together with the first paragraph.</p>

Headings

Earlier, you learned that the <title> tag does not really give you a big bold title at the top of the page. So, what does? It is the <h1> tag. Actually, the <h1> tag only specifies that you want something big and bold. It only goes at the top of the page if you put it right after your <body> tag. <h1> stands for a big heading.

> <body>
>> <h1>My Great Web Page</h1>
>> <p>This is my first Web page. I hope you like it.
>> I made it all by myself.</p>
> </body>

The <h1> and </h1> tags will make the words *My Great Web Page* appear in big bold letters at the top of the page (Figure 9.6). How big and how bold? We'll let the browser decide. The <h1> tag is all about specifying that something is a big heading and not worrying about the details (if you want to specify formatting details, you'll have to learn about CSS). Figure 9.6 shows you how this page will look in the browser.

Figure 9.6 Big heading using <h1> and </h1> viewed in the browser.

The <h1> tag is great, but you might want different levels of headings. For those you can use <h2>, which is a little smaller than <h1>; <h3>, which is a little smaller still; and <h4>,<h5>, and <h6>. Each heading will be smaller than the previous one. Just be sure that you use the same number with the close tag. If you have a <h4>, it must be closed by an </h4>.

Specifying Style

A fundamental difference between creating a word-processed document and a web page is who chooses how it displays, at least to a certain extent. In a word processor, the creator of the document makes all the choices; the creator chooses the font, its exact size, color, attributes (bold, italic, centered, etc.). Everyone who opens or prints that file will see the exact same document. HTML is different.

As noted above, HTML's h1 header doesn't specify details, it only tells a browser to use the size and styles it uses for h1. For example, a vision-impaired user may set his browser to show h1 as a giant font, perhaps 72 points—so large that only a few words can fit on a line. Another user may have a browser on her cell phone and prefer the h1 to be only slightly larger than regular text. Likewise, a colorblind person might tell his browser to display all clicked links as red rather than the default purple.

There are times when the web page designer wants to make sure everyone who views the page sees the exact same thing. Though there are a number of options for this, CSS is the most common. However, keep in mind that when you "force" browsers to display exactly what you want, you might be limiting who can use your page.

Linking to Other Pages

The <a> tag lets you create four different kinds of links: absolute links, relative links, email links, and internal links. The format is the same for each kind of link:

<a href="SOMETHING">

The tag for linking is the <a> tag, and the **href** parameter tells it where to link to. Remember: Different kinds of links all have this same format. The only difference is what goes between the quotation marks—in place of *SOMETHING*.

> **An absolute link** is a link to another web page somewhere out there. It requires that you specify the exact URL (uniform resource locator, also known as the address) for the page. The tipoff for the browser is that it generally starts with **http://**.
>
> > <a href="http://www.google.com/">This text is linked to Google.</a> This text is not linked.
>
> The latest editions of many browsers no longer show the **http://** in the address bar. Be careful. If you just type what you see in the address bar into your <a> tag, it will not work if the **http://** is missing. However, if you copy and paste the address, it usually picks up the **http://** so your <a> tag should be OK.
>
> As with most tags, the text between the tag and the close tag is what is affected by the tag. In this case, the words *This text is linked to Google* will be blue and underlined and be an active link when viewed in the browser. The words *This text is not linked* will not be an active link because the words are not located between the <a> tag and the </a>.
>
> **A relative link** is a link to another web page within your own site. This works when all the pages are in the same folder. The browser thinks that a link is a relative link if it leaves off the **http://**. In this case, you just include the name of the file within your own site (including the file extension) between the quotes:
>
> > <a href="other.html">Take me to my other page.</a>

This will tell the browser to look in the same folder as the page you are creating for another page named *other.html,* and the link will point to that.

An email link is a way to include a link that will automatically send an email. Using HTML, your email link will activate the default email program on the computer. If the computer is not set up with an email program (perhaps, you are in a public lab or you use a web-based email system), then a clickable link will not work. The browser knows a link is an email link because the part inside the quotes starts with *mailto:*

> **Send me an email by clicking**
> **<a href="mailto:marco@loyola.edu">here</a>.**

In this case, the word *here* will be blue and underlined and tell the default email program to send an email to *marco@loyola.edu.* If your computer is not set up to send email, it will be hard to test this.

An internal link can take you to another place within the document. This kind of link has two parts: an anchor and a link to an anchor. The anchor is a named location in the document. It also uses the <a> tag, but it uses the name parameter, **name=**.

> **<a name="dinosaurs">The Dinosaur Section</a>**

This tells the browser that this spot in the document is named *dinosaurs.*

If you want to link to that spot, you need a regular <a> tag with the part between the quotes starting with #. And you need to use the **href=** parameter to get it to make the link:

> **<a href="#dinosaurs">Learn about dinosaurs.</a>**

This link will scroll to the place named *dinosaurs* in this document.

Images

You can include pictures in your web pages. Generally, pictures on the web are in one of three formats: JPG, GIF, or PNG. You can get pictures by scanning them, taking them with a digital camera, creating them in a drawing or painting program, or saving them from other web pages. The key to saving pictures is to make sure that they are in the same folder as your HTML document.

To save a picture from the web, you must find a picture that you have permission to use. You can find pictures from copyright-friendly websites (such as http://classroomclipart. com and http://pics4learning.com) or search for pictures with a Creative Commons license (e.g., do an advanced search on http://flickr.com and check the box for Creative Commons). See Chapter Seven, Copyright and the Free Web, for more information about finding copyright-friendly pictures. When you find a picture you want to use, right-click, control-click, or hold the mouse button down on the picture until a menu pops up, and choose Save Picture As (or something similar depending on your browser). Be sure to save the picture to your folder, and pay careful attention to the name (you can change the picture's name if it is too complicated, but be sure to use a simple name with only letters and numbers), including the file extension (probably .jpg, .gif, or .png) because that is part of the name (if you change the name of the picture, don't change the file extension).

Once you have the picture saved as a file in the folder with your HTML document, you are now ready to go back to your HTML document and add the picture using the <img> tag. Remember that the picture is not stored in the HTML document; the <img> tag just points to the picture in the folder. Imagine you have a picture named *MyPhoto.jpg* in the same location as your web page. You can include the photo on your page with the <img> tag:

<img src="MyPhoto.jpg">

This is one of the few tags that does not require a corresponding close tag. The src parameter, **src=**, stands for source. The <img> tag can include several parameters, including **width=**, **height=**, and **align=** to set the width of the picture, the height of the picture, and the alignment on the page (left, right, or center). If you only specify width or height (but not both), the picture will be scaled appropriately without distortion.

<img src="MyPhoto.jpg" width="125" align="right">

The resulting web page will include your picture, *MyPhoto.jpg*, and scale it to a width of 125 pixels and align it on the right side of the screen with any text to the left of it.

Lists

Lists are a useful way to organize information on a web page. Lists either can be ordered (numbered) or unordered (bulleted). There are only three tags needed for lists: <ol>, <ul>, and <li>. Each list starts with <ol> or <ul> and ends with </ol> or </ul>, respectively. Each item in the list starts with <li> and ends with </li>.

For an ordered (numbered) list try the following:

```
<ol>
    <li>The first item</li>
    <li>The second item</li>
    <li>The third item</li>
</ol>
```

This will produce a list that looks like this:

1. The first item
2. The second item
3. The third item

To create an unordered (bulleted) list, change the <ol> to <ul> and the </ol> to </ul>:

```
<ul>
    <li>The first item</li>
    <li>The second item</li>
    <li>The third item</li>
</ul>
```

This will produce a list that looks like this:

- The first item
- The second item
- The third item

Lists can be nested by including lists within lists. Here is an example of a nested list:

```
<ol>
    <li>The first item is numbered 1.</li>
    <ul>
        <li>The first sublist entry is bulleted.</li>
        <li>The next sublist entry is bulleted.</li>
    </ul>
    <li>The next item is numbered 2.</li>
</ol>
```

This will produce a list that looks like this:

1. The first item is numbered 1.
   - The first sublist entry is bulleted.
   - The next sublist entry is bulleted.
2. The next item is numbered 2.

To make the nested list shown, you begin by creating a sublist after the first item. The sublist includes a complete list, namely a list starting with a <ol> or <ul> that includes one or more items (starting with <li> and ending with </li>) **and end**s with </ol> or </ul>.

Tables

Tables are the most complicated of the basic features of HTML. Tables are used for two purposes: to create tables and to line things up. Although many web pages use tables to line things up, this use of tables is discouraged in newer web standards (CSS is the preferred way to lay out a document).

There are three basic tags you need for tables: **<table>**, **<tr>**, and **<td>**. Every table starts with the **<table>** tag and ends with the **</table>** tag. Every row starts with a **<tr>**, and every item within a row (each data cell) starts with a **<td>**.

Here is an example with table tags:

```
<table border="1">
    <tr><td>one</td><td>two</td></tr>
    <tr><td>three</td><td>four</td></tr>
</table>
```

This will create a table that looks like Figure 9.7.

Figure 9.7 Four-cell table with a one-pixel border.

Notice the border parameter, **border**="**1**", which puts a border of thickness of one pixel around the entire table. For a thicker border, you can change the "**1**" to "**2**" or "**3**" or more. Note that as long as the border parameter is not "**0**", it will also put a one-pixel border around each cell in the table (larger numbers don't make the cell borders any bigger). Be careful that you always have a </**table**> at the end of your table. Otherwise, you will get very strange results.

The simple example for Figure 9.7 uses words in each cell, but anything can go in a cell. You can put a sentence, a paragraph, a list, a picture, or even another table in a cell. Just put the <**img**> tag between a <**td**> and a </**td**>, and you will have a cell with a picture.

```
<table border="1">
    <tr><td>one</td><td><img src="MyPhoto.jpg"></td></tr>
    <tr><td>three</td><td>four</td></tr>
</table>
```

This produces the same table as the previous example, but it replaces the top right cell in the table with a picture (assuming that the picture *MyPhoto.jpg* is in the same folder as your HTML document).

If the above example is confusing, try playing with it to see what results you get. You might also find it easier to understand if the various HTML pieces are on different lines (and indented).

The following HTML code is identical to the previous HTML code:

```
<table border="1">
    <tr>
            <td>one</td>
            <td><img src="MyPhoto.jpg"></td>
    </tr>
    <tr>
            <td>three</td>
            <td>four</td>
    </tr>
</table>
```

Resources for HTML

Freeman and Freeman's (2006) *Head First HTML with CSS & XHTML* is an excellent book that covers HTML as well as CSS. For online information about creating web pages, explore some of the following resources. There are many other resources in bookstores and on the web, so if none of these appeal to you, just look for another one.

Draac.com
http://www.draac.com

A website that includes easy-to-understand tutorials for HTML and CSS.

The HTML Code Tutorial
http://www.htmlcodetutorial.com

An extensive tutorial that covers basic and advanced features of HTML.

KompoZer—Easy Web Authoring
http://www.kompozer.net

A free open-source WYSIWYG tool for web page creation.

W3Schools
http://www.w3schools.com/css

An extensive tutorial about CSS.

Four-Step Process
http://tinyurl.com/WebPagePart1
http://tinyurl.com/WebPagePart2
http://tinyurl.com/WebPagePart3
http://tinyurl.com/WebPagePart4

The long URL for Part 1 is http://www.loyola.edu/edudept/facstaff/marcovitz/WWW/FourStepProcessVideos/WebPagePart1.swf

These four videos review the process for creating web pages in WordPad (in Windows) as described in the first part of this chapter.

Step 1. Create a document and save it for the first time.

Step 2. View a document in the browser for the first time.

Step 3. Make changes to the document and view the changes in the browser.

Step 4. Close everything up, go away, come back, and set everything up to continue editing.

Conclusion

This chapter has shown you the basics of creating an HTML document from scratch. Once you have done this a few times, you will have an excellent understanding of how web pages work and will easily understand any WYSIWYG web page applications that you encounter. Practice with HTML for a while, and look at some of the resources mentioned in the previous section to find more advanced features.

Exercises

1. This entire chapter is really an exercise. Go through the chapter step by step. Start by creating a simple HTML document with the basic web page directions given in the section titled Parts of an HTML Document. Save the document to a folder, and view it in your browser. Add more elements using the tags described in this chapter until you have a functional web page. Don't expect to be a master designer, but try to create something useful, if not beautiful.

2. Go to a web page on the web, and look at the HTML source (as described in the Why Learn HTML? section of this chapter). List all the tags you recognize. Find a tag or parameter you don't recognize, and try to figure out what it does by going back and forth between the HTML and the normal display of the web page.

3. Go to web tools that you use (or have read about in this book) and look for HTML mode in their editors. Many blog, wiki, and discussion tools allow you to type HTML into their editors, switch to an HTML mode, or add chunks of HTML without being able to edit the whole page in HTML (e.g., http://www.wikispaces.com lets you use the widget tool to add something with HTML). Use HTML mode to post something.

References

Freeman, E. [Elisabeth], & Freeman, E. [Eric]. (2006). *Head first HTML with CSS & XHTML*. Sebastopol, CA: O'Reilly.

INDEX

A

acceptable use policy (AUP), 3, 91, 162–163, 172–178

accuracy. *See* evaluating information sources

activity structures, 54–63, 77

    information exchanges, 56–58

    interpersonal exchanges, 55–56

    work and experiences exchanges, 58–59

    Internet as audience for writers, 59–61

    strategies exchanges, 61–62

add-ons, 9

Adobe Reader, 9

agnostic mode. *See* readers of the web, agnostic mode

All About Explorers, 23–24

Alliance for Childhood, 126–127

American Robin Migration Tracking Project. *See* Journey North

Animoto, 95

Associate for Women in Mathematics Mentor Network, 56

Atom, 102

Audacity, 95

AUP. *See* acceptable use policy

authority. *See* evaluating information sources

avatars, 97–98

B

Blabberize, 96

Black Invention Myths, 26–27

blog, 40, 59, 60, 61, 84, 86, 87, 88–91, 102, 108, 172–174, 188, 213

    acceptable use policy for, 172–174

    Blogger, 84, 91, 188–189

    Edublogs, 90, 91

    Kidblog, 91

Blogger.com, 84, 91, 188–189

bots, 127

browsers, 7–8, 195–197. *See also* reader of the web, browsers

bubbl.us, 21, 28, 84–85

Bullying Project, 72

C

calendar, shared, 101.

Center for Commercial-Free Public Education, 127

checklists. *See* evaluating information sources, checklists

Children's Internet Protection Act (CIPA), 169–170

Citrix, 106. *See also* cloud computing

classroom clipart, 150, 207

climate change, 29–39

cloud computing, 105–108

cognitive miser, 18, 19

Columbus, Christopher, 23, 39

Common Sense Media Programs, 178

Commons, the, 143–145. *See also* Creative Commons

Copia, 101

context, 25, 26–28

copyleft, 133, 142. *See also* Creative Commons

copyright, 3, 131–157. *See also* fair use; Creative Commons

    permission, 138–139, 146–147

    public domain, 137

    songs, 137

    United States Copyright Office, 136

    work for hire, 138

copyright symbol ©, 136

coverage, 22. *See also* evaluating information sources

Creative Commons, 3, 131, 132–134, 137, 142–155, 207

    licenses, 146, 147, 149

    music and sounds, 150–151

    noncommercial, 147

    pictures, 148–150, 207

    searching for, 133–134, 148–152

    sharing work with, 143, 152–154

    some rights reserved, 145, 149

    and student-created work, 155

    symbol, 146

    text, 151–152

    videos, 151

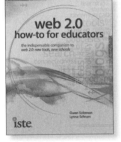